Mill House

Mill House

by

Sue Blow

Ella Publishing

First published in the United Kingdom in 2002
Reprinted in 2004 by Ella Publishing
CA13 9HQ

Copyright © 2002 Sue Blow
Illustration Copyright 2002 Sue Blow

ISBN 1-904515-01-0

Printed and bound in Great Britain by
Athenaeum Press Ltd., Gateshead, Tyne & Wear

Mill House

The writing of Mill House is my interpretation of family members personal memories. I apologise in advance for any unintentional variance in my story telling.

I would like to thank the family for all their help and patience not forgetting my husband who pays the telephone bills!

Vera Leighton 1942

Preface.

"Mill House" was written for our granddaughter, Saskia, who was born in Brussels. With better education and in most cases, an immensely higher standard of living, our children leave us to travel for work, happily not war. The consequences being that they settle overseas and have their families. Many of us are no longer parents living around the corner or in the next village. Precious holidays spent together with so much to say and so little time to say it in. The grandchildren obtaining snatches of family history from very often already elderly grandparents because their parents had them later in life, to accommodate the professions that they studied so long and hard for. Our son was born in York which makes Saskia a European with Yorkshire roots! Also Austrian and Dutch roots too, a true European!

Chapter One

Mill House

I have been told that it was a bright sunny day, the day that my grandparents Emily & Alfred Leighton moved into Mill House with their three children. The year of 1926 in a village called Newport, in the East Riding of Yorkshire. They had moved only a short distance along the road, a road that ran alongside a canal. The canal was cut in the 1700's to give access to the barges to serve the local brick works and the farms along its route from the River Humber up to the lock at Holme-upon-Spalding Moor and later Market Weighton.

There must have been a great deal of excitement surrounding this move from a small cottage to the five bedroom spacious house with its many out buildings. The house was built in 1900 by the Darling family who were the owners of the windmill. A solid looking house, built in the red brick of the area, double fronted with long narrow windows. Windows that in the upper rooms at the front of the house came nearly to the floor, giving good views of the canal and in the near distance the village main street. None of the village shops on this street could be seen from the house and the canal had to be crossed by a bridge when going shopping. At this point in time the bridge would only have been wide enough to accommodate the passage of a single horse and cart, not as robust as the two that have subsequently been built.

The Darling family obviously thought that the wind mill had had its day and for some reason demolished the mill and its sails in 1924 leaving only the base of which had been the engine and boiler rooms. The granary, which stored all the grain to be ground, was only a stones throw away across the yard. The Darlings had decided to sell and move to a larger farm to accommodate their family. In those days most farming families tried to supply their offspring with employment on their own land.

At the beginning of the 20th century great numbers of Scots, Welsh, Irish and farming families from the North of England emigrated to America and Canada where they hoped with hard work they could better themselves. Alfred had four brothers, two of these Herbert and Arthur went out to Canada with some of the first immigrants, later taking Canadian citizenship. By 1912 they had persuaded Alfred to join them and he also became a Canadian citizen. Alfred settled very near to his brothers on the island of Schugog and we believe at first worked as a farm labourer for a German couple.

Unfortunately, events at this time are very vague but we do know that it was only a short time before the First World War was declared and Alfred joined the Canadian Scottish Highlanders. Why no one seems to know, maybe it was the distinctive tartan of the Black Watch that had something to do with it! Many years later, Alfred's eldest son was to join the Royal Scots Fusiliers.

Alfred set off from the island of Schugog with his regiment to train on the shores of Niagara, a spectacular training ground. From these shores they received a tremendous send off from the local people and this stayed with Alfred to the end of his days. From here to war - in France! It was while fighting in France that Alfred lost his left eye at Vimy Ridge and was sent back to hospital in England. Overnight, twenty four hours after losing his eye, Alfred's thick hair turned pure white.

After the war he and members of his regiment received a heavy gold ring each with an inscription from the islanders and two half sovereigns as well as military medals. Alfred also received compensation for the loss of his eye and being a Canadian citizen, a Canadian pension which in years to come benefited him because of the good exchange rate with the dollar.

It was during this time in England recuperating that he decided not to return to Canada but to again join his family in the East Riding. His parents, Annie and Joshua, were living at Sandholme near Newport. My great grandfather, Joshua Leighton, was well known all over the Ridings of Yorkshire for his expertise in sheep shearing and I understand was never known to be beaten in a contest.

Shortly after his return Alfred met Emily who was nine years his junior and fell in love. Emily was the daughter of Minnie and George Coultish and was born at Broomfleet Landing in East Yorkshire. All these place names ending in " Landing" were places where the bargee's would stop and take the cattle being transported to graze and be watered, transporting animals were on occasion lengthy journeys. The land that runs along the banks of the river Humber is extremely fertile, below sea level and was reclaimed by experts from Holland who had managed through engineering to hold back their own seas. It was from this good soil that most of the population in this area made their living. The village of Broomfleet lay peacefully along the banks of the canal, approximately one and a half miles inland from the river Humber, winding its way through Newport and eventually into the Wolds of the East Riding.

Emily had nine siblings, six brothers and three sisters. At the age of fourteen Emily left school to begin her working life. Girls from her background where given little choice and usually this meant working on the land or going into service. Emily worked for a local family of butchers and farmers called Kirk and I believe was very happy there, she was treated as one of the family. It was whilst at work that she met Alfred.

Alfred who was born in 1890 had four brothers and four sisters. The sisters were Lily, Annie, Kate and Laura. Laura married a German gentleman after the First World War and later emigrated to America. Lily married and moved to the market town of Beverley in Yorkshire, later having twelve children and was then known to the rest of the family as "The Old Woman who lived in a Shoe," the nursery rhyme goes on to say, " so many children she didn't know what to do!"

In 1918 Emily and Alfred were married. Their first home was a small cottage on Canal Side West, Newport. In the time that was to follow Alfred would have little time to think of Canada as their own family and business ventures took over.

Their first born was George who appeared early in their marriage followed shortly by Lily in 1920. My own mother, Vera, was the next to be born in 1923. During this time as well as the children coming along there had been much thought, saving and planning going into the decision of buying a property, also what sort of work would suit them both and give them a good living to provide for their growing family.

Two suitable properties came on the market at the same time, only a matter of yards between them. Both would suit the requirements that were needed being five bedroom properties. Each property came with land and out buildings and both were on the side of the canal with only a small row of cottages between them. The other property did not have the open views that Mill House enjoyed, but its garden ran down to a large pond which was rather picturesque, but also rather hazardous when there were small children in the family. Decisions had to be made, savings assessed. Of course, no one can be sure but most of the family seem to remember that it was Emily who made the final decisions about most ventures. From what I understand my grand-mother was an extremely ambitious, hard working lady who idolised her children and always made sure that they had the best. There were never any photographs taken of Emily so the grandchildren that sadly were never able to meet her have only their own images as to what she looked like. Taller than most women of her time I remember being told, with dark hair cut into a tidy bob. Emily had drive and foresight and Alfred I believe had a gift for maths, extremely unusual at that time, obviously taking after his own father and grandfather who had a reputation in the area for water divining and the sinking of wells. Apparently, he could calculate the materials needed with a pencil and paper in only a few seconds much to everyone's surprise. Alfred and Emily made a wonderful team.

Chapter Two

Moving In

The removal day must have been exciting, exhausting, frantic and even frightening for Emily who was still only a very young woman with three small children under her feet. The thought of furnishing this, what must have seemed to her a very large house, would I think have been at least a little daunting. Emily had plans involving a lot of hard work, but this didn't worry her.

Alfred had already gone into business as a coal merchant not long after their marriage. One of his sisters, Annie, had married a pit manager, a very prestigious job. They lived at Grimethorpe in the West Riding of Yorkshire, only in the next county but in those days travel was very slow. My mother and her brothers and sisters can remember visiting their aunts and uncles in different parts of Yorkshire but no-one can remember their mode of transport! Alfred had a love of horses and the coal was, for the first few years delivered by horse and cart.

Moving into Mill House must have made life easier in some ways even, though the land and property would need attention. Nancy, Alfred's first horse had been purchased from the army after the First World War, as Alfred had been in the cavalry this appealed to him. After a day of pulling the cart she now had a large roomy stable and lush paddock to graze in. Apparently it was common to see Nancy taking it upon herself to move onto their next customer if Alfred lingered longer than she wished while on their rounds. In fact, Nancy was very frisky and temperamental but from what I remember of my grandfather he wouldn't stand for any nonsense for long. Emily and Alfred also decided to rent a local field as Emily had a wish to own a small dairy herd. The pig sties needed stocking, hens for the hen houses, and geese to be acquired. There was one thing that was always certain at Mill House, there was never any shortage of food.

Emily watched Alfred from the kitchen window leading Nancy out of the stables to be hitched up to the waiting cart. He cut a very dashing figure, not tall, only a modest five feet seven but firm in muscle because of the physical work that came with his occupation, most of the year supporting a tan because of the time he had to spend out in the open. His thick, snowy white hair and eye patch covering the empty eye socket, gave him an air of eccentricity. Alfred was in fact a bit of a ladies man. He had worn a glass eye for several years but dirt, dust and wind caused aggravation, hence the patch.

As usual the kitchen was the hub of the house pleasantly heated in the winter from the ever burning black lead range, a huge looking monster to a child looming over the kitchen, taking up lots of wall space in width and height. Filling the corner space between this and the wall was a large brick hot water boiler also heated from the fire to be used for filling the tin bath or other household chores.

The open fire with a swing rack over the coals usually had a kettle or pan perched upon it, simmering on the boil. On one side of the fire a large oven that was permanently heated and on the other a small chamber holding water that meant a constant supply of hot water was at hand. There was a water pump in the opposite corner of the kitchen positioned over a large stone sink which in those days was a modern convenience as it saved having to go outside in all weathers to fetch water. There was also a long narrow table fixed to the wall under the window. Emily would spend hours standing here baking, preparing vegetables etc. over the coming years. A Windsor chair and several other chairs filled the rest of the room. Whenever Alfred appeared, whoever was occupying the Windsor chair vacated rapidly.

A corridor ran from the back door to the front door cutting through the middle of the house, opening up into a square hall at the front entrance. Across the corridor from the kitchen you entered the dairy which I would describe as a very spacious larder. Descending four steps then led you into what was known as the far dairy, where all the sides of bacon etc. were kept after the slaughtering of a pig. It was strategically placed and very cold even in the hottest of summers.

Back to the kitchen side of the red quarry tiled corridor and into the living room, square and light, as all the rooms at the front of the property were. The outside wall of this room housed the chimney breast and fireplace, a large wood surround inset with Victorian painted tiles and above a modest mantel with a mirror. Floor to ceiling cupboards furnished one of the recesses next to the chimney breast. These cupboards, as I remember, housed a treasure chest of china and ware objects, including a large tea and dinner service in Cottage ware. It was always a great treat to me as a little girl just to have the cupboard doors opened and be able to gaze upon these wonderful little cottages, to look was enough, to handle would have been to much of a responsibility, I realised even as a young child. The other recess had a window looking onto the drive at the side of the house. Out of this room and turning towards the front door you would enter the square hall with all its coat pegs on one wall to be much used in the coming years.

The front door had two glass panels in the upper section, again letting in the southern light. Across this hallway one entered the front room, the main feature being the fireplace, beautiful wood with a spectacular mantle reaching nearly to the ceiling. This incorporated small cupboards with minute keys to lock them. How these keys didn't get lost is hard to imagine they were so small, tiny cupboards in which to lock tiny treasures away from tiny people with clumsy fingers. Back into the hall, up the open spindled wooden stair case to the first landing of which were the first two good sized double bedrooms, these both being at the rear of the property. Climbing another short flight of stairs to the next landing off which where the two main bedrooms, in between which was a much smaller room. Alfred and Emily occupied the first of these rooms, a beautiful room, square and very light because of the lengthy windows. There was a small fireplace in this room as there was in the other mirrored room across the landing.

What impressed you on entering the small bedroom was the view of the garden that seemed to take up the whole of the facing wall. There was only room for a single bed down one side of this room. It must have been a real pleasure to wake here and inspect the day, whatever was in store. As a child, an only child, I remember sitting on the sunny staircase and day dreaming about all the hustle and bustle, laughter and tears that the walls of this house must have absorbed over the years.

Chapter Three

Day To Day Chores

Everyone had settled well at Mill House except for the first few days when Vera, then two years old, had to be taken back to their old cottage to use the toilet. Luckily, this hurdle was soon overcome as it was time consuming walking backwards and forwards usually meeting friends, neighbours or relatives who would enquire about their move.

There was, of course, very little plumbing in the 1920's and most people had earth toilets, no electricity and in the country, no gas. Paraffin lamps and candles were used in the house and a lamp called a tilley lamp or storm lamp was carried when going outside to inspect the stables or out houses.

Emily could not remember a summer being hotter, it was with sheer relief that she thought of the autumn and the days becoming cooler. It was the end of August 1926 and she was again pregnant, the heat may well have felt more intense because of her condition. Her chores seemed never ending from rising early to milk the cows she had acquired, getting the children George and Lily ready for the village school, feeding the poultry and pigs and then starting the general house work, while all the time keeping her eye on Vera.

Luckily Vera wasn't a mischievous child and would be very happy following her, helping or amusing herself. Once the children had gone to school and the stock had been fed, the fire tended, Emily would set to her many other tasks. If her day wasn't well planned she would literally run out of time before her jobs were completed. One of the jobs Emily most disliked was done on a Monday, wash day! The wash house, only a few yards from the back door and yet not intrusive, was a real luxury as most people had to do their washing in a cramped kitchen or even an outside back yard, but there was still a great deal of hard work involved.

Water had to be carried from the outside pump in the yard to fill the huge boiler, which often had to be coaxed into staying alight. The dolly tub, a metal barrel shaped container filled with hot water and soap in which the washing was placed and then beaten in an up and down movement with a dolly stick. A very strenuous job, especially for someone who was pregnant. A long wooden washing trough stood on a sturdy stand in which you leant a wash board, where extra dirt and grime would get an extra scrubbing on the board or with a scrubbing brush.

Women's hands would be harder then because of all the manual tasks, they had cracked, painfully sore hands most of the winter months. After the process of boiling the white garments in the boiler and all the scrubbing and rubbing they were then rinsed in clean water before being put through a mangle. An ugly looking metal and wood contraption with large wooden rollers put into action by turning a wheel on the side. The clothes then passed through the wooden rollers and a good deal of the water was squeezed out of them. Fine wash days were a bonus especially in the winter and the children would dread returning home from school in the bad weather knowing that they would find the kitchen fire obscured by clothes horses hung in wet washing. Even the ceiling would be out of sight as a wooden pulley was also overloaded with these wet garments. Steam would fill the kitchen and the smell of soap would fill the house, on such nights nowhere ever really got warm and a dampness hung everywhere.

Weather permitting the clothes would be put out on the washing line to dry. Having an expanse of open drying area to Emily was a real delight, as in the past she had had to manage with a limited space, in their previous cottage's back yard. The sun only managed to penetrate this yard in the height of summer. While all this was in progress the kitchen fire had to be kept alight, heating water for the house and the oven, ready to cook the evening meal. Mondays usually meant cold meat left from the Sunday joint, roast potatoes, scrubbed and cooked whole in their skins and whatever vegetables were in season. A fruit pie to follow, there wouldn't be a great deal of choice in pies after the weekend, when everyone had been at home and working up their appetites either working on the property or putting energy into playing!

Tuesday always meant a big baking day, a meat and potato pie made in a large enamel bowl, curd, fig, apple, gooseberry pies or whatever fruit was in season. In the winter these pies would be made of preserves in large glass jars in the autumn or from apples stored in boxes wrapped in paper to help prevent them going rotten. The fire oven made the best milk puddings ever! With milk straight from the cow, rice, sago, pearl barley cooked slowly tasted really delicious and the children would fight as to whose turn it was to have the crispy skin that had formed over the top.

Chapter Four

Help At Hand

In the early weeks of September Emily became extremely tired carrying her fourth child. On the 29th of September 1926 their third daughter was born, Mabel, named after Emily's younger sister. There had been great celebrations earlier in the year when this sister had been married from Mill House. A family gathering, but when you are one of ten siblings, large numbers are easily reached! Emily had six brothers Alfred, Arthur, George, Fred and Ernest. George sadly had been killed in the first World War. The three girls were Violet, Gladys and Mabel. Their modest family home at Broomfleet had always felt as if it would burst at the seams if all the family were at home at one time, Mill House still felt quite spacious with their own four children. Before marrying Mabel had left school and gone into service, to work for a family in Welton, E. Yorks. A village twelve miles from their home, both Emily and Mabel had been very lucky in their employers and had been well treated and appreciated. Mabel was now to move into her own home, Emily had lent her one of her treasured possessions, a suitcase that she had won showing one of her rather too well looked after pigs! Walter Waudby, the happy bridegroom, was the son of a strong Methodist farming family living in South Cave. South Cave and Welton are pretty villages on the edge of the Wolds with good farming soil.

Their home, built in wood, was a perfect picture book cottage, fronted with a veranda, which in the summer months cascaded with climbing roses. Walter loved flowers and a number of their acres were put over to growing tulips for their bulbs. People would travel from miles around in the spring to see the colourful acres of blooms.

Mabel, the new addition to the family was a happy and contented child. Darker in colouring than her siblings, very like her namesake. When she did as all babies do and demanded attention her older brother and sisters were more than pleased to assist.

Lily's first thought after this birth of yet another sister was only of concern, another head of hair to put into rags every night before bed! Emily was most particular that all her girls were well turned out and that meant the tedious job of winding rags around sections of the long hair to produce a ringlet when released of them the following morning. Emily was pleased after her confinement to get back into routine, but not for long.

Vera now four years old was suddenly taken ill, out of the blue. The local doctor, who was also their adjoining neighbour was called and rheumatic fever was diagnosed. The acute fever that followed was alarming for Emily and Alfred and caused concern for several days until the worst passed. It was going to be a long slow progress for Vera to regain the use of her limbs as it had left her with acute stiffness in all her joints. There was a fear that the infection would cause lasting heart problems. Vera was a strong child and well nourished, which may well have saved her life. People would use remedies passed on by previous generations, as calling out or visiting the doctor cost money that many of them did not have. It was a common sight to see Doctor McKenzie riding around the village streets on his old bicycle piled high with garden produce, eggs and even a chicken or two in payment for his services. Luckily, Emily and Alfred were not in this position and they thanked god.

Times were particularly hard at this time in Britain as they were in the grips of a general strike which caused more hardships and poverty. Because of living in farming communities country children were often better fed and therefore had a much higher chance of recovery after illness. Emily didn't realise how tired she had become and couldn't have managed as well as she did without the help from kind friends and relatives.

Across the yard the upper floor, above the granary and two coach houses, which were all part of the Mill House property had been a private school, run by an elderly lady called Miss. Bullan. When she retired and closed the school Alfred let the premises as a flat to a Mr and Mrs. Williams and their only son, they owned the fish and chip shop in the village on the main street. As close neighbours Mrs Williams did what she could to help with the other children while Emily was nursing Vera through the worst of the fever. Alfred's parents had by this time moved from Sandholme and were living in the end cottage of the row where the young couple had started their married life. Other neighbours fetched the cows up from grazing to be milked and returned them and generally helped where they could. George was also becoming a great help, Emily was very proud of George's school work. In fact both George and Lily were always at the top or near top of their classes at school. George loved music, singing and dancing and was taking violin lessons at school, he was a well built child but very light on his feet and always chosen to take part in any country dance festivals that the school attended.

15

Therefore, it was again unexpected, when George complained of pains in his legs, it was usually thought to be "growing pains".

It was expected that children who were growing would experience aches and pains of some sort and it was put down to the fact that they were growing too fast, whereas the reason would be that there was a lack of vitamins and minerals in their diets. This shouldn't have been the reason in George's case as the table at Mill House was always more than well stocked. Again the doctor was called and Emily was told that George had acute rheumatics. Nothing at all to do with Vera's rheumatic fever as they had feared. The family was only just getting back to normal after Vera's illness and now George's illness was a great shock. His legs gave him a lot of pain and he didn't have the strength to stand for a number of weeks, and yet he wasn't unwell in himself. He hated missing school and after only a short while at home persuaded his mother to take him. So as well as all her other responsibilities Emily carried him on her back to school, returning at break time to take him a drink of egg and milk to build up his strength.

After several months George returned to normal and the family sighed another sigh of relief. George always spent a great deal of time with the animals at Mill House and several of these became very attached to him. One in particular, a wild duck! This duck would follow George everywhere including going to school each morning, so instead of carrying George to school Emily often had to go after him and retrieve the duck! Eventually the duck had to be penned up until George was out of sight. Life is never dull with animals and children and Emily had plenty of both.

Chapter Five

Furnishing The Home

Spring was now here and everything looked brighter, it was drier under foot, which made life more pleasant, the children could run in and out without constant trails of mud and dirt.

During the winter months Alfred and Emily had made the decision to rid the outside brick work of the house of the invasive clinging ivy, this was to be a major job. Once this was done the house looked vulnerable, stripped of its lush foliage wrap. Work began probing, poking and scraping out the old mortar, making the house look sad and uncomfortable. Gradually the fresh mortar was neatly coaxed into place and suddenly "Mill House" took on a look of pride and confidence, as if proudly greeting it's inhabitants as they gazed at the neat workmanship. The old ivy overcoat forgotten for its trim, new look.

At last, with the family in good health and the sun shining for weeks on end, Emily found time to take stock of her home which was at last coming together satisfactorily.

One person in particular had made this possible, a Mrs. Robinson who owned a shop on the main street. The shop stood under the village clock and Mrs. Robinson sold anything and everything. It was a friendship that grew over admiration on both parts. Emily admired Mrs. Robinson, an elderly lady who had achieved her wish to run her own business making a good living, Mrs. Robinson recognised herself in the young hard working woman.

Mrs. Robinson enjoyed acquiring furniture for Emily nearly as much as Emily enjoyed receiving it into her home. Most of the pieces were obtained from the sale rooms in the city of Kingston Upon Hull, the nearest large town to their village.

The city of Hull was at that time the third largest port in Britain, with fine tree-lined avenues where the wealthy merchants lived. Many of these houses were furnished with articles brought from foreign shores and occasionally these pieces found their way into the sale rooms, the most prestigious of which was Gilbert Baitson and Son. This family later became life long friends of Emily's sister, Mabel and her husband Walter Waudby.

Mrs. Robinson was a frequent visitor to these sales and well looked after by the staff. Emily only had to express her wish for an item of furniture and Mrs. Robinson was on the look out, very often picking extra items that took her eye, knowing that Emily would appreciate them. One of her most exciting finds was a large bedroom suite, thought to be French and in Birds Eye Maple, beautiful pieces comprising of a huge double wardrobe with full length mirrors, chest of draws, dressing table and a marble topped wash stand. The workmanship and finish is unobtainable today. Other pieces that brought special delight were two pianos - one for the front room, and one for the living room. The superior one, of course, went in the "best room," this had marquetry insets and fitted candle holders all rather grand.

The second piano more modest, had far more use in the living room, only to be played properly by none members of the Leighton family. After many lessons it seemed no one had the gift of playing the piano. I am told that a large amount of money was spent on lessons for the children but they were all relieved when the elderly lady giving these lessons decided that she could no longer make the journey from her village on her bicycle. I wonder if the lack of musical talent of the Leighton children had anything to do with this decision!

A wonderful set of cranberry coloured glass bowls adorned the front room piano, I believe they are called "Epergne," in the antique world. Had this glassware been placed on the piano in the living room they would not have survived, as the piano was played with great gusto by the younger members of the family and their friends. This room also housed a pair of crystal bowls, their edges hung with detachable prisms, so when the sunlight danced upon them they captured every colour in the rainbow.

A frequent visitor to Mill House was a young girl called Elsie, who visited her grandmother Mrs. Bentley. Her cottage garden ran along the bottom of the Mill House front garden, a garden that Alfred kept well tended. The lawn was like velvet with two diamond shaped flower beds either side of the front door. In the spring these beds would be full of spring bulbs followed by wallflowers, snap dragons, asters and dahlias.

The front garden was the one place that the children would not venture to play in. Elsie was slightly younger than Vera and as there was little age difference between Lily and Vera the three girls spent a great deal of time together. Falling in and out of friends for much of the day, Sunday being one of these days as they went to Sunday school together. They all belonged to the Primitive Methodist church where Elsie's grandmother was a much respected teacher and in later years Vera was herself to supervise the younger children. The Sunday routine was to get their jobs out of the way as quickly as possible, get ready for Sunday school which involved dressing in their best clothes, a great effort for them all but if they were honest with themselves made them feel proud and walk tall.

An annual event that caused great excitement was the trip by bus to the east coast seaside town of Bridlington, it meant an early morning start but there were never any complaints. Five buses would leave Newport and set off in convoy along the country lanes towards the sea. Their excitement would rise as their destination grew nearer, each and every child hoping that they would be the first to set eyes on the North Sea. Great cheers would vibrate around the interior as their controlled excitement began to loose its grip.

With great relief to the adults in the party once the sea was sighted there was only a short distance to travel . As soon as their vehicles parked up the children poured out with their buckets, spades, balls and tiny wooden boats, whatever the weather they headed straight for the beach, leaving the more senior members of the party to struggle with the more mundane items of discarded clothing etc. Weather permitting a picnic lunch would follow and if they were lucky ice creams and donkey rides along the beach.

The day would pass all too quickly and there would be an air of sadness as they boarded the buses for their return journey home. Sing alongs would momentarily lift their spirits as gradually the younger children gave in to sleep, eventually all the occupants becoming quiet with sheer exhaustion. The children took a lot longer to vacate the bus than that same mornings exciting boarding, they now struggled to their feet and had to be virtually pushed along, unenthusiastically gathering their belongings as they departed. It was only on the return to their own homes that recalling some of the days events to a family member that had been unable to make the trip that the memories of the day sent them happily to their beds, to dream of the following years outing. The anticipation being as pleasant as the event.

Chapter Six

An Unusual Purchase

After a great deal of thought Alfred decided he would have to invest in a new cart for the business. After attending many local sales and making extensive enquiries Alfred purchased a cart and "rully" from a retiring green grocer in Kingston upon Hull. When first approaching the seller Alfred could see no use for the canvas covered wooden structure covering the cart called a "rully", but as the negotiations proceeded and the bartering got under way the elderly gentleman did not realise Alfred had bought the cart and cover for his original offered price, not to include this covered structure! The poor man had been no match for Alfred!

There was to be a big surprise for Emily and the children. Alfred approached the local joiner and told him of his plans. The "rully" was lifted from the flat bed of the cart and placed along the side wall of the warehouse and coach houses, in full view of the kitchen window. It was to have a strong wooden base, sides, windows and doorway, even a chimney for ventilation. Several people made remarks as to whether this was to be Alfred's new home! As the work progressed the excitement grew, the children hardly dare think that this little hut that was changing daily into more of a miniature house could be for them. But it was, and to the three little girls it was a dream come true. They would have moved in with their beds if they had been allowed. Curtains went up, rugs on the floor, chairs and a table. Even a stove for when the weather turned cold. Elsie was allowed if she would bring her wind up gramophone! In the next few years Elsie and her gramophone would be in and out of the little house like a yo-yo! Emily could not believe that Alfred had instigated this project as the children where usually the last thing on his mind, she gratefully appreciated his thoughtfulness as she now knew exactly were all the girls where most of the time which gave her piece of mind.

A Mrs. Lupton from Hull caused great excitement at Mill House, this lady travelled to the villages carrying her huge cases of clothes for all the family, household linens including bedding towels etc. but it wasn't these items that interested the young girls. They would try and sit still until the mundane business was over and then it would be their turn to delve into the treasure trove! Emily knew exactly what she wanted for her girls and these garments usually had to be ordered and brought on the following visit as Mrs. Lupton's stock was more of the utility than feminine underwear etc.

These frivolities were much thought of by the girls while doing their chores, however young the child, they had their little jobs to do. Whitsuntide was one of the main dressing up events of the year and they all looked forward to wearing their fine new clothes. They were, however, always aware that not all children were as lucky as them-selves and could feel quite guilty when noticing the look of envy on some of the other children's faces.

Emily was easily persuaded by the girls from a very young age to purchase rather more feminine items than was the norm and they could at times be very cruel to Elsie over her red flannel bloomers and layers of red flannel petticoats. The finest of their outfits came from an unlikely source, a Miss Donna, who owned the village Post Office. None of the sisters can remember, or knew where these garments originated from and after having to wait several weeks for these orders to be realised there was too much excitement to care.

As the summer months faded and winter drew in the girls would be measured up for their annual velvet dresses. They all remember their beautiful rich colours, the soft texture and fine needle work. They also remember the soft wool coats and matching bonnets. Black patent bar shoes complemented their outfits. In the summer their dresses would be of lighter material accessorised with a chic straw bonnet or boater tastefully trimmed.

Spring brought another pleasurable pastime after Sunday school and their usual tasty roast dinner. They were then allowed to change into playing clothes and with friends wander down the lane past their grandparents to the brick works, to play! A horrific thought today, all the hidden dangers. No-one remembers any accidents, I am sure there must have been a few, if only minor. Part of their time would have been spent picking the wild flowers that were in abundance, riding in the trucks on the rails. The trucks were used to move the clay often on the edge of the extremely deep clay ponds. It does not bear thinking about.

There was a great difference in the ages of the children that collected for this Sunday pastime, so one can only surmise that the more sensible, not always the eldest, kept some sort of control. These deep ponds and wild surrounding were the ideal habitat for otters to breed and this brought otter hunts to the area.

The children would watch these huntsmen in their smart red coats, congregate on the banks of the canal before proceeding with their hunt. The girls would not follow this sport any further as they found it too upsetting.

Chapter Seven
Many Hands Make Light Work

1928 - The four children now ranged in age from two years old to ten years old. All the family were kept busy from dawn until dusk, the eldest of them taking it in turns to accompany each other in bringing the cows up from where they had been grazing, from the opposite canal bank to be milked by their mother. They then had to deliver milk to their customers, all before going to school which was no easy task for young children, particularly in the depths of winter. Occasionally they would have a shortfall of milk in the winter months, but farmer Kirk was more than happy to make the measure up for them. Alfred in exchange would help on the Kirk's farm during harvesting, when his coal business was quiet.

The children's friends would offer to walk with them when the weather was good but volunteers were thin on the ground in the bad weather. Lily had a friend that loved to accompany her when delivering to an elderly gentleman called Mr. Wightman, he had a never ending collection of scary ghost stories. Both girls would encourage these stories and then rush home frightened out of their wits, only to return within a few weeks for a repetition.

Another cheery customer was the owner of the public house only a few yards from their own home called the Crown and Anchor. Very few people had spare cash to treat the children when it came to the Christmas delivery. The children were aware of this but nevertheless took great pleasure in receiving any that were offered and the owners of this public house made a point of giving each of them a small gift. Every evening, whatever the weather, you would see old Mrs. St. Paul strolling up the lane with a jug in her hand going to collect her beer. This elderly lady always wore a man's cap, which made the girls giggle. The family dog, a terrier called Spot would trot along by the side of this village character, wait for her to get her jug refilled and trot back with her to Mill House where the old lady would then continue on her way. Spot occasionally went missing for a few days which troubled the children but he never came to any harm and eventually died of old age. Alfred favoured terriers, one of the reasons being that they were classed as working dogs and therefore did not require a dog licence. Alfred didn't like to part with his money unless absolutely necessary. During one of Nancy, the horse's spirited performances, she ran straight into the path of a car, cart and all which was an unlikely occurrence as at that time there were so few cars on the roads, Nancy was as shocked as the driver.

Weeks of confrontation followed as the car driver expected compensation from Alfred but there was no way that Alfred was going to take the blame and said "That it was an act of God." Once Alfred had made up his mind about anything there was no moving him and this caused several battles of wills between him and his off-spring in the years that followed.

Chapter Eight

Visiting Relatives

The girls took turns in going to spend a few days holiday at South Cave with their Aunt Mabel and Uncle Walter, usually in the good weather. My own mother remembers missing home but it was a welcome change from rising so early to fetch the cows and take out the milk. Aunt Mabel had no children at that time, but they did have a fluffy little Pekinese dog. He wasn't as cuddly as he looked though and didn't appreciate the children's company.

Uncle Walter played the organ in church and he was also a Methodist Lay preacher. They had an organ in their own home and Walter would play at any opportunity though not very often in the summer months when pressures of work were greatest working on the land. Many people associated the Waudby's home with musical events as over the years they entertained many Yorkshire brass bands that were playing in the area.

An Aunt Kate and Uncle Jack who lived in Hessle were also visited. They had bought their own house down a tidy Avenue off the main road from Hull to Hessle. The houses had been built by a local co-operative and at the time had cost £300 which in those days would have been a great deal of money and calculated as a high risk purchase to most ordinary folk. Kate was a small framed lady with a happy, pretty face and she and Jack had three sons. Sadly their eldest son, Herbert, had died in an accident at a young age after falling from a cart while playing. Their holidays at Aunt Kates were always enjoyable and she appreciated the girl's company. The neighbours children welcomed them into their games and it was a good excuse when visitors came to have a game of tracking, which involved drawing arrows on the pavement to show the direction you were heading in, then to be tracked by the rest of the party. This game didn't go down too well with some of the other residents, but a good shower of rain soon put things right and washed away the chalked arrows.

There were picnic trips to a local beauty spot called "Little Switzerland", an old disused, quarry on the side of the River Humber that had become overgrown with trees and wild flowers, to a child with a little imagination it was quite magical. They would set off with the picnic basket packed with goodies, make their way towards the main square in Hessle and then turn off one of the roads towards the foreshore, past the haven where ship building and fitting would be in progress and onto one of the grass or pebble tracks that ran along by the side of the river Humber.

The Humber estuary did at that time carry heavy shipping, bringing cargo from all over the world, reloading in our ports of Goole and Selby with steel and coal. If the tide was low and the day was hot the mud flats could smell quite unpleasant, the plus factor of this was that cobbles could be thrown and spun across the mud, each child competing for the highest score.

During the summer months when these picnics usually took place the paths along the river banks were lined with wild Budleagh bushes, in the heat of the day the perfume from them would be wonderful, masking the unpleasant odour from the mud if the tide was low.

After passing the shipyard and following the track they would come upon a very large house with undulating lawns and gardens that ran down to the foreshore. The house had been a nunnery, an impressive looking building with ironwork balconies to the upper rooms overlooking the estuary and in the distance the Lincolnshire countryside. Little did Vera know that in future years she, her husband and daughter (myself) would live in this house. The nunnery was eventually sold to a company called Earls Cement. Vera's husband would work for this company and be one of the first tenants to move into this unusual home that would be converted into tastefully, stylish flats for their employees.

The area became wilder after passing the neat village gardens and tended fields full of ripening crops. All the party had worked up a good appetite by the time they arrived at "Little Switzerland." Finding the actual place to picnic always took some deciding, in or out of the sun, near the pond and the flies or back near the cliffs. What decisions! Compromises were usually made quickly as everyone would want the picnic basket settled on the ground and the goodies displayed as soon as possible. The basket would contain a home made pork pie, boiled eggs, home cooked ham sandwiches, buns, biscuits and home made lemonade. There would be at least six children on these picnics, on some occasions one of Kate's neighbours would accompany her with her own children. It was a long walk to this over grown old quarry and the children, especially the younger ones found it a struggle to walk home. The older boys of Kate's would end up having to piggy back the youngest of the party home.

Kate was very grateful after these outings, the evening that followed seemed most tranquil and quiet, no-one grumbled when bedtime came around.

Kate and Jacks' boys were good company, and to the girls they appeared "worldly," different to the village boys. Hessle was not a town but to the girls it might just as well have been, there seemed to be so many shops and they loved the atmosphere, hustle and bustle around the main square. It was always good to return home, even to the early morning chores and routine tasks that had to be carried out. When first away on these holidays the girls enjoyed the break from their siblings but as the days went by they became unexpectedly missed!

On one occasion whilst Vera was staying at Grimethorpe with her aunt Annie and uncle Frank one of her cousins Marjorie fell ill with scarlet fever, this meant that Vera and her aunts other daughter Dorothy had to be in quarantine for two weeks. Vera thought the two weeks would never end, to everyone's relief neither of the girls contracted the disease and Marjorie made a complete recovery.

Chapter Nine

Fast Moving Seasons

Into the year of 1929, the business, family and home had all improved for the better. The children were all at school and doing well, Mabel had now grown from a placid baby into a dreamy, easy going child who seemed happy in a little world of her own most of the time. Vera who was just the opposite loved this younger sister but did on many occasions find her most irritating. Mabel, day dreaming, not rushing at anything, dropping her clothes and leaving them lying around anywhere. Vera always in a hurry and relatively tidy found this difficult to handle. Mabel didn't notice! Lily's character was a well proportioned mixture of both her younger sisters and in later years was the one that the family would tell their troubles to. In return Lily would in most instances confide in Vera.

During the winter months Emily had planned the oncoming spring clean. Mrs. Bentley their neighbour would as usual be called in to do any wallpapering that was needed. This lady was a good friend to Emily and helped her in many ways. The spring sun light that streamed through the windows made the constant hard work that went on in the house seem worth the effort. The children could once again play outside, as well as in their play house, which meant they would no longer be under Emily's feet.

George spent much of his time with the animals and it was at about this time that he acquired his first ferret. This ferret and later others were housed in the pig sties. At one time George was surprised to find one of his nesting ferrets had given birth to ten young. Lily and Vera didn't take to these small sometimes vicious animals but Mable loved them and would beg George to take her to play with them. His two elder sisters would much have preferred him to give more time to his other passion of collecting cigarette cards. George still remembers today at the age of eighty his pleasure from these cards and in return exchanging them for picture prints. A print of a horse and foal was his favourite and he kept it for many years. Emily found it hard to keep up with George's many interests. He would be involved with practice for the choir, the school dancing troupe or violin for some forthcoming function or other. Any other spare time would be spent with his pals or the animals, George's days were never long enough.

The girls would spend hours playing with their celluloid dolls that had been in their Christmas stockings. Mrs. Bentley had worked her magic yet again in turning these plain celluloid dolls into wonderful replica babies for the girls play. On Christmas morning they would willingly rise early contrary to the other 364 days of the year, race to the foot of their beds to find some much sort after toy or game plus a chocolate novelty in the form of a football for George, dolls for the girls. Emily went to great pains to find these items for the children and the pleasure seen on their faces made it more than worth while. Many children at this time would be lucky to receive a piece of fruit and a hand made gift.

In later years the children would partake in spending part of their Christmas morning accompanying their Headmaster, carol singing at the workhouse in Howden. The children would return home very subdued but once enveloped in their security at Mill House the festive spirit soon returned, the children never forgot those poor people that unfortunately were not as lucky as themselves.

As the seasons moved into spring and the cold frosty mornings gave way to bright warm sunshine inside pursuits were forgotten for more outdoor activities. My mother and aunts told me of showers in the spring where it actually rained tiny, tiny frogs! It would in fact be the geographical placing of the great expanses of water in the area that made the tiny young frogs to be washed onto the roads and made so visible. I remember thinking that it must have been magic!

After the spring showers the air would hold wonderful pockets of perfume around areas of primroses, violets and bluebells. Vera particularly loved the violets and along with her sisters was allowed to go into butcher Kirk's orchard and pick a posy to take home for their mother. The arrival of the first baby chicks would be anxiously awaited, adults and children alike watching the athletic antics of the little balls of bright yellow fluff. The girls would play hop scotch, skipping and bools while George was usually to be found with the animals if not doing jobs for his father.

The house would be turned upside down, cleaning, papering and painting. Emily had another reason for wanting to get the house spick and span, she was again pregnant and the baby was due in the coming October. Emily realised that she would have to be more organised than ever, if that was possible, to keep the business going and not drop any of her standards.

Chapter Ten

The Black Sheep

Winter, spring and into summer, time went by so quickly. There had been great excitement when George went with the school choir to sing in York, quite an honour for a small village school. The school sports followed soon after, an event that all the Leighton children looked forward to taking part in. Vera proudly held the cup for several years before leaving school and with three other pupils travelled to Malton in Yorkshire to represent the East Riding. These events were shortly followed by the local show which brought visiting relatives from the surrounding villages, some not as welcome as others! One not unwelcome but caused Emily some anxiety was Fred, Alfred's younger brother. He was the black sheep of the family, a real character, all the children loved him. He and Alfred wouldn't be together two minutes before they would be falling out and he would be told to pack his bags and move on! He was full of fun which appealed to the children but not always very responsible.

Alfred's parents now lived a few hundred yards down the canal bank from Mill House and Fred would go there out of the way if he thought he had pushed Alfred too far over one subject or another, usually politics! Alfred was right wing conservative and Fred was left wing labour, It was an entertaining sport for Fred to goad Alfred on this subject in particular. Fred enjoyed winding people up and then he would disappear as quickly as he had appeared, on his bike usually wearing shorts whatever the weather, leaving every one feeling very much worse for wear after his visit.

Newport show had come and gone, the harvest was almost gathered in and Emily was well into her pregnancy. The children were all getting excited about the coming event, the girls of course more than George and on October the nineteenth 1929 Alfred and Emily became the proud parents of yet another daughter, Nora. A beautiful baby that every one adored. After the birth Mrs. Robinson purchased a pram for Emily, a very fitting pram for such a bonny child with a pink lined hood and body. Nora looked the perfect little rose nestling down on the white broderie anglaise pillow case and matching sheets.

Emily had shared her confinement with a friend of hers, Esme. Esme and her husband Jim had for a short period lived at Mill House until they found accommodation after their marriage, later moving into Jim's parents small holding after their deaths. This young couple would certainly have their hand's full as they had twin daughters.

While this couple were living at Mill House it was arranged that Esme would take Lily with her into Hull for the day and while there Lily would have her long hair styled and cut. This was to take place at a salon called Meeks, which had an excellent reputation but was known to be expensive. Lily's excitement grew over this secret shared with only her mother and Esme. After a wonderful day they returned home and everyone exclaimed their surprise and delight, except Alfred who was furious. Even at school Alfred insisted that the girl's hair stay long and loose, this had meant that their hair fell onto the desks as they worked which hadn't pleased the teacher. Nor did it please the teacher that Alfred would not let any of his children visit the free school dentist.

Lily now nine and Vera six would proudly push their baby sister up and down usually with the assistance of Mable now three. Nora was much more exciting than their celluloid dolls! At that time no-one knew of the excitement the following years Newport show would bring, when Nora would win the "Bonny Baby" competition. These events were always well supported, entrants for competitions high.

A routine was again established and another Christmas was upon them which meant that there would be another stocking this year to be filled. Though still only a tiny baby Nora's stocking would have to be evident or the other children would want to know why Father Christmas had excluded their sister. Some time during the month of November the children would walk to a local wood and collect cob nuts as the start of their Christmas preparations. The family all remember the days leading up to these Christmases long ago as great fun with the air full of anticipation.

Preparing for the school pantomime made for enjoyable lesson times, it was a very unexpected event when Vera, the shy one of the family took the lead part of Aladdin in her last Christmas at school, her slim build and height making her an excellent choice. Mill House would be enveloped in seasonal smells of boiling puddings and roasting meats, all the shelves in the dairy would be heaving with the extra festive food that had been prepared. One of Emily's specialities was curd pies with a seasonal touch of dark rum, to keep out the cold! More than seventy years on today my mother can get quite nostalgic when thinking of this tradition of their mothers. A few days before Christmas Eve the children would decorate a tree, make paper chains to hang from the ceilings and decorate the house with holly and seasonal greenery.

George now going into his twelfth year was quite a young man doing well with his schooling and a great help to Emily and Alfred. Lily and Vera were also enjoying school and all the activities attached to it and Sunday school. These two eldest sisters in the family were great friends as in the future Mabel and Nora would become. No-one ever had time to be bored, their chores had to come first and then what ever project was happening at the time would be given attention, often by the whole family.

Alfred's business was doing well and Emily had built up a sizeable milk round with her dairy cows. The other livestock on the farm were of excellent stock and with good feed and husbandry were considered at showings as first class. George took particular interest in the many different breeds of chickens and later in his life bred and showed unusual breeds all over the country, attaining many cups and trophies.

The children's grand parents had now moved out of the end cottage that they had bought and into a wooden prefabricated bungalow in the grounds of the cottage orchard. Alfred's youngest brother George and his wife Edna were now living in the cottage. Canal Side West had a good number of Leightons as residents!

The brick works was only a few hundred yards away from this row of cottages and as a good number of the employees lived on the opposite bank of the canal the employers rigged up a flat boat to give them easier access. This flat boat was attached to a chain in turn attached to each bank, as the chains were pulled the boat would automatically be floated across the canal to the opposite bank.

Children were not encouraged to use this transport but of course that made them more intrigued and inquisitive, periodically youths would have to be chased off. Everyone knew everyone else in the village which made identification easy and a parental scolding would be awaiting the offenders, which in those days could be very grim.

Chapter Eleven

Annual Events

Children are attracted to water, as are a great number of adults! With the canal running through the very centre of the village it was obviously a great part of their lives, used for commerce serving the brick works and farms but also for their leisure including fishing and events such as boat racing and water sports day.

Most of the villagers enjoyed this event, as most people enjoy seeing someone else get a thorough wetting. Activities during the day would include climbing the slippery pole in which the local policemen took part, and a pig tub race. The pig tub was a small wooden, flat bottomed boat shaped trough that was used to place a pig in after being slaughtered. These troughs had no stability on water and caused much hilarity for the spectators as the competitor battled to keep afloat. The hostelries on either side of the canal enjoyed these events as trade benefited especially if the weather was pleasant and families picnicked on the banks whilst watching the activities.

As these events took place on a Saturday the holiday mood would carry on into the evening and night with a dance in the village hall. Sunday mornings came round all too soon, especially for the young people that had to rise early and tend to the animals on the farms. Many felt that they had been hit over the head with the slippery pole and that the dance band from the previous evening was resident in their head, or at least the drummer! The young villagers worked hard and they played hard.

One of the last events on the calendar for outside activities that the children looked forward to was the night stopover of a very large travelling fair. This was the second largest fair in the country next to the Nottingham Goose Fair and this stop would be made as the fair made its way to Hull for the annual event afterwards proceeding on to Nottingham.

This event took place the second week in October and made a welcome distraction from another seasonal activity that was not as pleasant, potato picking! An occupation that made most peoples' backs ache and their whole bodies become stiff and uncomfortable with the constant stooping that had to be done to obtain the potatoes. At this time of the year the weather is most unpredictable in England and over the period needed to harvest the crop the pickers could be in brilliant bright sun shine one minute and torrential rain storms the next. Whole families would partake in this boring job which has become easy now with mechanisation. It was a way for them to make a little extra money, often put aside for Christmas.

There was great excitement awaiting the fairs arrival from early on in the morning the day that the fair was expected and many of the children would walk way out of the village, then rush back as soon as they had seen signs of the approaching fair.

Villagers gathered as animals, carts and covered wagons congregated on the banks of the canal. The biggest attraction never changed, "big", being literally big - the elephants! Young children would stare in disbelief as these huge creatures waded into the canal to bathe after their tiring walk, the sizes of these beautiful animals varying from the bull down to the youngest offspring. Most of these children would never get to the real Hull Fair or a circus ring but this spectacular site of animals and colourful people more than outweighed the rehearsed circus acts. The Leighton children found it hard to tear themselves away from all this activity and when bedtime came they would creep out of their beds to peep out of the curtains and watch the surreal goings-on right outside their own home. It was like a dream, in the glow of the camp fires, the shadows of animals and people, many resting after their hard day. The time passed too quickly and the travellers and their animals would be on their way early the next morning leaving only the flattened grass, wheel ruts and a little litter to show of their presence.

Alfred had admired several of the horses belonging to the fair folk and now looking at Nancy he decided it was time to let her retire and have a well deserved rest, she was becoming an old lady and had a full working life. So the search for a new horse began, Alfred would not be easy to please!

Several months on and Blossom had been purchased, a beautiful chestnut mare who was bought from Atkits farm in Holme on Spalding Moor. Blossom was later to produce a foal that was Alfred's pride and joy, sadly this foal had a tragic end when he ran into a piece of farm machinery whilst being chased by youths. Youths then as of today still do not realise the implications of their actions until it is to late.

Chapter Twelve

Family Confinements

Every day life went on in the usual routine, including Emily's pregnancies! A slight difference with this pregnancy was that Emily had company in her confinement. Mabel, Emily's younger sister was at last expecting her first child, everyone breathed a sigh of relief when she delivered a healthy baby boy who they named Donald. Ethel, Emily's sister in law who only lived a few hundred yards down the canal side was also pregnant for the first time and on Feb 15th gave birth to a beautiful little girl, Brenda. Exactly three months later on May 15th. 1932 Emily gave birth to their second son, Alfred was ecstatic.

This new addition to the family was to be named after one of Alfred's elder brothers in Canada, Herbert. The " Mill House" family were not a tactile family but there was no doubt of feelings of being loved and wanted, and Herbert was certainly wanted, especially by his father. Alfred had the old fashioned view that girls were all right in their place but caused worry and expense!

Emily did not regain her former strength after this pregnancy, it was not just this pregnancy but the accumulation of previous pregnancies that told on her health. Walking became increasingly difficult and the eldest children took on more chores and helped were they could.

The strong character of Emily shone through as she tackled things in any way that she could, surprising every one as she adapted herself and her family. Luckily no-one was to know at that time that Emily would never walk properly again. My own mother still remembers the last walk that they all took together as mother and children to visit Emily's parents and grandparents in Broomfleet. A long walk for the younger members, along the canal bank, but a very pleasant one on a fine warm day. The children could run and skip into the distance without Emily worrying about danger of horses or traffic. They had been well schooled in the dangers of the canal and farm machinery.

As young as the children were instinct seemed to tell them of how much their mother appreciated them being responsible and how it helped her with her disability. Emily pushed Bert in the pram, occa-sionally taking Nora on board as her legs tired, while all the time using the pram for her own support.

Emily found the return journey a great struggle and was to never tackle it again. As the months passed it became more apparent of Emily dragging her leg, Alfred kept hoping that things would return to normal.

A rocking cradle was made which spent most of its time beneath the kitchen table where Emily could sit and rock with her good leg while preparing vegetables or baking etc. Tasks became more difficult for Emily but with her organisation and the help of her family things went on as near to normal as possible. The children did at times of course take advantage of the situation and would push their luck with their replies to their mothers remarks, moving quickly out of her reach!

42

Emily soon became aware of this tactic and acquired a long handled hair brush, she would give them a sharp tap when they came back within her range! Emily remained very much in control.

Alfred's youngest brother George and his wife Edna whose daughter Brenda had been born in the same year as Bert and lived a few hundred yards down the canal side, they would call in to see Emily and the children on their way to visit the village shops. Brenda was a happy, bright child with an abundance of blond curly hair, Emily's children loved her.

As Brenda grew she would spend as much time as she was allowed at Mill House with her cousins and her auntie," Emply." Brenda found it impossible to pronounce Emily.

It was unusual to approach Mill House and not hear the sound of children at play, the orchard and large yards attracted the children from neighbouring cottages. Nora had a little playmate called Davy, they had been playing outside together one fine day when Emily heard an abrupt knocking on the already open back door, accompanied by a quiet crying.

Immediately Emily made her way to the door as quickly as her disability would allow her, to find a neighbour who ran a small sweet shop from the front room of her cottage a few houses along the road. Nora and her little friend, both around the age of four had called at the shop, chosen sweets and given the lady chocolate money in payment for their purchases. The shopkeeper was not amused! Emily found it hard to keep a straight face, until looking again at the children's tear stained faces. It was now Emily's turn to be not amused and told this person in no uncertain terms what she thought about the way that she had handled the situation. The little shop lost substantial custom over the coming months.

The years moved on and Emily's condition grew worse, the only way that she could get from one floor of the house to another was to go up and down stairs on her bottom. To move around at all became increasingly difficult, having to sit to do all her jobs. The children adapted and knew exactly what was expected of them, none of them resenting the extra jobs that had to be done. George was now fourteen years old and looking forward to leaving school, he was also to get his first pair of long trousers, at this time it was a momentous event in a young mans life. They were to be made by the local tailor Haige. George worked as his fathers right hand man, Lily taking on her mother's work quite naturally. Vera doing the domestic chores expected of her, but not as easily as Lily and Mable fell into them. Vera being a different character in many ways, preferring her own company when possible, even eating her meals apart from the rest of the family when she could.

Vera concentrated more on her schooling, other village children would refer to her as being a "snob," this didn't worry her as she found conversation boring with her own age group and confided closely with her mother. Emily in return understood this daughter wanting to reach further than the average village youth, she had shared this same feeling but hadn't had the chance of the education that she hoped to give her own family. Mabel and Nora constantly cheerful, with good imaginations spent happy hours in a pretend world of their own. Bert also a content toddler had plenty of attention from his sisters. All in all no mother could have asked for more, except the importance of her own good health.

Chapter Thirteen

The First To Fly The Nest

Summer 1932 - George left school at the age of fourteen and for several months he worked for his father. The following year he was offered a position for a company of contractors working in the East Ridings of Yorkshire area. It was at the time a big decision, as it would mean George living away from home all week returning only at the weekends.

George decided to spread his wings and accept the position, leaving home at 4am on a Monday morning on a three hour bicycle journey and returning on another three hour ride the following Saturday afternoon. Monday to Friday nights would be spent in lodgings. After working from 7.30am on a Saturday morning until early afternoon George would pray for fine weather for his journey home, the dark winter months making depressing travelling, all the family would wait anxiously for his return. George was greatly missed at home, not only by Alfred and Emily but also by his older sisters and younger brother. One of George's old school friends called at Mill

House each week with a quarter of a pound of buttered brazils for Emily, which she found very touching and greatly enjoyed.

Most evenings it would be nearly midnight before Emily finally made the strenuous journey up the stairs to bed. Dragging herself to the first landing and then onto the second of the two steps leading into the first bedroom at the top of the stairs. Mable, Nora and now Bert shared this room. The two girls shared a double bed, Bert still occupied his cot.

Bert was going to be a child that would have to be moderately restrained, as still only a toddler he was as quick as greased lightning!

Putting Bert in with the girls had been a good move on Emilys part as both girls would chatter well into the night, with a baby in the room this made for complications, if Bert woke up they would have to pacify him. Easier said than done!

Emily looked in on her sleeping children, their profiles showing clearly on moonlight nights as the cotton curtain material was of no weight. Noticing the repaired bed leg she laughed to herself, she certainly wished she had their energy. They had been up to their usual high spirited tricks one evening before Bert had been "billeted" with them jumping up and down on the bed doing "Ann Driver" exercises. Ann Driver was the equivalent of our Green Goddess today. They had exercised with such enthusiasm that a leg had broken off the bed, excitement soon turned into anxiousness as to what their father would have to say. Which was not a great deal, what the girls got up to was beyond Alfred, he didn't understand them and was sure he never would.

Emilys next port of call was the bedroom across the landing occupied by Lily and Vera. These two older daughters would also whisper together well into the night. Emily was grateful that all her children got on so well, not all families were so lucky. The last tiring stage of

Emilys journey to bed meant tackling another four or five steps to reach her own and Alfred's room. George's room was next to their own, the door always stood ajar while he was away from home. Every night that his room stood empty Emily would say a quiet "good night" to her absent eldest son before finally retiring herself. The only other door on this landing belonged to the guest room, another beautiful large, light room that Emily loved but sadly she rarely ventured into any more.

Lily was now due to leave school and it was decided, after great discussion, that she would remain at home. Alfred had suggested they get a local woman to help Emily but Lily was very happy to stay and help bring up her young brothers and sisters, this was done automatically by Lily. This troubled Vera as it would not have been her choice, had she been offered it.

The subject was discussed frequently by Lily and Vera, Lily convincing Vera that it was not against her wishes. Emily felt very relieved with Lily's help as her younger sister Gladys had been cycling from Broomfleet in all weathers to assist with heavy tasks such as the washing. This worried Emily, her nature was strongly independent.

It tore at her heart to see her family getting on with life at such a speed, she felt that she could only watch from the side lines.

Nora and Bert loved having Lily at home to help take care of them but Lily was more agile than their mother and would soon bring them to task as Emily had been unable on occasions to do so because of her immobility.

Bert had a friend the same age as himself who lived a few cottages away from his grandparents and aunts and uncles on the canal side, they called him Sam Marwood. Sam was a chubby cute child with very fair curly hair, every one wanted to mother him, he looked as if butter wouldn't melt in his mouth! Sam was full of fun and mischief.

Emily spent a great deal of time wondering what Bert was up to while in the company of Sam. Not that Bert wouldn't get into mischief on his own, but he and Sam together made for double trouble!

Vera was now following in Lily's footsteps at school, not always as easily as she had expected! Lily was a quiet, easy going girl but always ready for a bit of fun. In the last two years of the girls schooling they would attend a domestic science course held at a much larger school in the neighbouring market town of Howden.They would travel by the local bus along with other people going to work in the port of Goole, or further.

Another regular passenger to use this transport was a local journalist for the Goole Times. This colourful gentleman was a real character and was known by everyone as, "Wiggy Haynes," as he wore a very obvious ginger wig. He regularly reported the girls to their head master for making too much noise! When they arrived at Howden the class would be made up with other girls from schools in Eastrington and Hemingbrough.

Vera was soon to find that Lily had not been one of the teachers' favourites, this particular lesson had given many opportunities to get up to harmless mischief, such as sneaking into the pantry and eating the appealing provisions. When Lily's year of girls had their last lesson they collected together to buy the teacher a present. Lily and her friend, Florence Jackson anonymously bought an extra present and wrapped it up very well, a large wet, pungent prawn! Their teacher was not amused and had a very good idea of the group involved.

In Vera's last year at school she travelled to Edinburgh on a school day out. There were very few pupils whose parents could afford to let them partake in this venture, consequently the party was small and they were able to see more than had it been a larger group. Vera was very impressed with what she saw, promising herself to return in the future. Previously George, Lily and Vera had all gone on an outing to London with the school. London Zoo was included in the sight seeing, as the last stop of the day. When it was time to board the bus George was found not to be with the rest of the party. Lily had an idea, and she was right. They had a job to drag him away from the elephants!

Chapter Fourteen

Difficult Decisions And Tragedy

DEATH OF GEORGE 5TH-------ABDICATION OF ED-WARD-----CORONATION OF GEORGE 6th

Visits to aunts and uncles continued for the children, as family continued to visit "Mill House," concern for Emily grew. One regular visitor to the house was a Herbert Fielder, who called at the house every month to take Alfred's order for the coal wholesaler. Over the years Herbert had become a family friend and had a midday meal with them at each visit, talking over a wide variety of subjects as this rather refined man had many interests. The girls had been most impressed when Herbert had married and bought his new bride a Musquash coat as a wedding present! He followed the children's progress with great interest as he had known most of them from birth, his admiration for Emily grew as the years went on and he witnessed her struggle and dogged determination.

Emily could no longer put her head in the sand, she had to think of making life simpler. Parting with her beloved cows would help as the work connected with them started early in a morning and went on well into the evening. George was now away all week and so tired on his return home it was hardly fair to burden him with more than absolutely necessary. Lily had her hands full with the younger members of the family, Vera helping before going to school and also on returning. Regardless of their difficulties it remained a very happy household, until February 14th. 1936.

There had been a very bright, cold spell and everywhere had been dry and crisp for several days, on such days the children gathered to play outside. There was a feeling of excitement amongst the Leighton children, Brenda their cousin was to be four years old the following day. She had called in at Mill House to see her lovely aunt "Emply". After visiting Mill House and giving her usual update on the progress of her now nearly one year old brother, Maurice, she had gone on to the village shops to purchase items for her coming party. Full of fun and chatter as usual she continued on her way, waving and shouting as she passed again on her return home.

This bubbly little cousin always made them smile with her sheer enthusiasm for life. But what a short little life it was to be, later that very same day the dreadful news reached Mill House that while playing in a boat (totally out of bounds) with two little male friends on the edge of the pond in their own garden Brenda had lost her footing and plunged through the ice into the freezing water. It was later diagnosed that Brenda had suffered a heart attack from the freezing cold. Sadness gripped the family for months, obviously Edna and George never got over losing their daughter.

Emily found herself going into a deep depression and decided now was the time to make the changes that she had not looked forward to. Life must go on and she was going to make it as easy as possible. Her dairy cows must go, they would be missed by all the family.

There was however to be an addition to the work force, after much discussion Emily and Alfred decided it would be in their interest to purchase a vehicle for the business. A very unusual purchase in those days, Emily didn't think that she would ever see the day that Alfred would chose mechanics over his passion of horses. A passion he was never to lose. Alfred became the proud owner of a Ford lorry, bought from a market gardener in South Cave. He then had to take a driving test in the city of Hull, which he passed the first time. Emily was very proud of him. This purchase would cause quite a stir locally and was the main topic of conversation for many a month.

In the years that were to follow Alfred often looked back with relief as to when he made this purchase. In the coming years questions were asked as to how people that had previously appeared to have no spare cash suddenly acquired expensive possessions! In the future Alfred was given many opportunities to make easy money but he would take no part in such dealings. However awkward and stubborn he could be, he had his principles except maybe where paying his taxes were concerned! On several occasions he received summons for withholding payment and was threatened that his goods and chattels would be removed! Emily would be horrified, intervening and paying the debt immediately.

Vera was now approaching fourteen and would shortly be leaving school, Emily had always been proud of her daughter's ability and hoped that she would continue to study.

It was while this subject was being discussed on one of Herbert Fielder's visits that he mentioned his wife's former time spent at the private secretarial college in the city of Hull called "Gregg School." The girls were carefully selected and after completing their time at the college were held in high esteem. Lengthy discussions followed and Emily and Alfred contacted the college. After a glowing reference from Vera's Newport school it was decided that Vera would attend the Gregg School, paying the fees for one year.

This was to be a totally different world for Vera, travelling to and from home by train each day into the city. Still a shy girl, it would not be an easy step for her to take but her common sense and confidence in her own ability would get her through. Vera would board the train at Wallingfen, it would take her ten to fifteen minutes to walk alongside the canal and then take a path that ran along the railway track. The trains were well used in this area and very often full with passengers, not to mention the animals and unusual cargo to be found in the guards van! Goats, rabbits, pigeons, bicycles, the guards' vans were spacious and if the commodity fitted this was the way that people would transport it, cheaply and reasonably quickly. Vera soon got to know the regular travellers, and would meet other girls that went to the same college as herself further along the line. Dorothy Turpin, Dorothy Parkinson and Audrey Marsden would get on the train at North Cave and before they knew were they where it would be time to end their journey, with still an awful lot of girls talk having to wait until their return that evening.

Veras time passed happily and quickly while at college. Life fell easily into place, each lunch time she would take a short walk to have her lunch with some old friends and neighbours, Mr. and Mrs. Williamson that had been her fathers tenants in the school flat at "Mill House."

Mr. and Mrs. Williamson had run the fish and chip shop in the village at Newport but had since moved into the city. They had a thriving business in Osborne Street in Hull, the offer was made that Vera should spend her lunch break with them. This suited Vera as she loved fish and chips and the Williamsons were particularly good. Alternatives would be offered, but not accepted. Mrs. Williamson had been a good friend to Emily and the two women sent their news to each other through Vera.

The principal at the Gregg School was a one armed gentleman, Vera guessed in his late fifties called Mr. Dawson. Normally it would take twelve months before the pupils would be summoned by him to, "collect your hat." This would mean that the particular student was thought ready to take their place in commerce and gain practical experience with the company that at that time was looking for a new employee. Vera had only been studying eight months when this request was made, Emily was of course extremely proud of her daughter's achievement. Vera's placement was with a large furniture retailers called Harry Jacobs, in Hull, it was a family business with fifty employees.

Life looked rosy, but not for long. Emily had felt content with all her family settled and happy. The one thing that Emily dreaded happening had happened, she was yet again pregnant. It would have been difficult for any woman in her late thirties whose family numbered six already. The thought of the actual confinement in it's self without the after care of a new baby unnerved Emily, for the first time in her life she felt that she could not cope. Fear was constantly at the back of Emily's mind, a feeling that she was not accustomed to.

Emily wondered if her prayers were being answered when she felt the excruciating pains in the lower part of her body. Events happened rapidly and before Emily knew what was happening she was on her way to the Hedon Road hospital, in Hull with Vera following, being driven by a family friend. Emily had a miscarriage, her feelings were divided. If only she had her health things would have been different. The only good thing about the hospitalisation was the rest that was imposed on Emily. Her spirits were also lifted when told by one of the doctors that she may in the future regain the use of her leg. Luckily, Vera was able to visit her mother in her lunch breaks and when George returned home at the weekend he arranged that his friend, Jim May, drive himself and Vera to visit their mother. The look on Emily's face as her two children approached her bed made their hearts leap, their mother looked more relaxed than they had seen her for a very long time.

Much to Vera's delight she became a permanent member of staff at Harry Jacobs in the New Year of 1939.

This was going to be a good year Emily told herself, still hoping every day to have less pain in her leg and more mobility. Sadly it was not to be. Emily became racked with pain and had to take to her bed, the doctor came and said that there was nothing that could be done. Emily passed away in March of 1939. I have not pried too deeply into this event as all my contacts, Emily's children now ranging from seventy into their eighties still find it too emotional to recall in any detail. They all remember the same thing, the cries of pain from their beloved mother.

Emily was laid to rest in the village churchyard, the three younger children recollect being taken for a walk by their uncle George. They walked down the side of the canal while the funeral took place, in the distance they could see the main road and the long funeral procession. Emily would be remembered and missed by a large number of people apart from her family.

Life would never be quite the same at Mill House, as Emily was "Mill House."

Alfred became quieter and short tempered, he spoke to Lily only over concerns of the house or the children. George returned to work away, Lily took on her mother's role as much as she was able. Vera had kindly been given a week's leave by her new employers, but was now returning. The younger children continued to do what young children do, but missed their mother unbelievably.

The family struggled through the summer of 1939 in a daze, although with great concern of the unrest in Europe. Reports on the radio did not sound good, but country folk continued with their everyday lives and when the sun shone one could for a while at least imagine the world was at peace.

"Mill House" saw changes in the first quarter of the year, who could have foreseen the changes that were to come!

Chapter Fifteen

Great Changes

September 1939. War had been declared. Official posters appeared everywhere, representing every governmental department possible from the Armed Forces recruitment advertising to the National Savings Committee saying, "Put it in the bank, it'll help buy a tank."

Events happened so quickly people hardly had a chance to draw breath. George was in the first draught of young men to be called to fight for his country. These young men where called, "Militia boys." When George received his official call-up papers he had to report to Doncaster, a town in the South Riding of Yorkshire where he had a medical. Shortly after this George had to report to a camp in Ayr, Scotland. These young, " Militia boys," had no uniforms or kit.

The regiment that George was placed in was the Royal Scots Fusiliers. What a dashing uniform it was when at last the lads took possession of them except that George thought that the legs on the trousers were a little too tight for his liking! Never one to waste time George arranged for a local lady to let out the seams down the legs of his pants as much as she could, he was very surprised when he ended up in rather a lot of bother and the legs of the trousers immediately narrowed again!

George didn't look for trouble but nevertheless it seemed to find him, not long after the trousers incident he was summoned to the Duty Officer in charge and asked if he was getting sufficient provisions. George replied that he was, why then asked the officer was George receiving food parcels from home that were large enough to feed the regiment. Lily and the girls took it as part of their war effort to keep George healthy and to them that was to eat well, these parcels contained home cured hams, home made pork pies etc. Lily at this time, now nineteen years old could side a pig as quickly and as well as any man, a feat her father was proud of.

There was to be yet another tragedy, concerning the local young couple that had stayed at Mill House before the war. It affected the whole village not only the family and friends of Esme and Jim. Jim's pigs had contracted Swine Fever, all of his stock had to be slaughtered. No one had foreseen the effect that it was to have on Jim. Several years after the birth of their twin daughters they had celebrated the birth of a son, Tony. This small boy was idolised, particularly by his father which made the events that followed seem even more surreal.

Sadly Jim murdered his son, he was convicted and later spent a long time in Broadmoor prison for the mentally disturbed. Many years after the sad incident Jim visited Alfred at Mill House.

Only a few weeks into the war and the family company that Vera worked for decided to stop trading. All young men were being called to fight for their country and the last thing that was going to be on peoples' minds was to refurbish their homes. Taking everything into consideration the family had the unenviable job of finishing all their staff, a very sad day for all concerned.

Vera had been so happy there she now wondered what awaited her, she didn't have long to wait. It was brought to Vera's notice that local government offices at Hailgate House in Howden were extending their facilities because of the war. A Food Office to deal with rationing and permits was to be an addition in the building. Vera immediately applied for a position and after having to go before a board of interviewers was offered a placement. The interviewers had been the local doctors wife, several local business men's wives and Mrs. Scofield of Sand Hall.

The gentleman that was to be the head of the Food Office was a Mr. Green a local solicitor and clerk of the council. Vera was very grateful for the position, but not too sure how she would handle the bike ride that she would have to make each day! Vera and bicycles did not get along together too well! Over the next few years this journey was made daily in all weathers and when caught out in an unexpected thunder and lightning storm Vera would quickly abandon the bike anywhere and head for the nearest house for refuge, so great was her fear of thunder and lightening. This phobia has never left her.

Lily was very troubled that one morning she would receive her call up papers in the post, inevitably it happened which at the time caused much concern because of the role that Lily was now taking in the family of still young children.

Vera asked the advice of Mr. Green, her new employer, who could not have been more helpful. He gathered as much information as he thought relevant, even offering Lily a job at the Food Office which would relieve her of official military duties. Lily declined the kind offer, even though her father offered to get help in the house, nevertheless she was pleased that she had such an understanding and respected gentleman standing her corner. Lily's case went before a tribunal in Doncaster and with great relief to all the family Lily was excused military service.

Everywhere Lily looked she would see the advertising posters to help with the war effort, she would do all she could to play her part. Many of the posters were based on humour, British of course! One such poster read, "Always have food for bombed-out people that is easy to eat. The first thing people lose are their spectacles, and the second is their teeth."

Alfred wondered if their family life may now resume some normality, some hope! In the coming years Alfred would think on occasions that he was living in a circus. He would even think that it maybe easier to take Hitler on single-handed rather than try to understand his four girls, how he missed Emily.

There were going to be spectacular changes in Europe, also "Mill House." Alfred was about to fight his own war, sometimes with hilarious consequences, often tinged with drama.

Alfred's two eldest girls had become friendly with a group of young men from the village of South Cave. Vera's first brief taste of romance was with a young man called Frank Donkin. A good while after this relationship faded away, Vera received a Christmas present sent anonymously. The present was a beautiful squirrel skin evening bag, which she liked to think was from Frank, but she never did find out.

The two sisters also enjoyed playing tennis and whenever possible they would put on their whites and make their way to the tennis courts at the village hall, on the recreation field. Mabel and Nora would watch them set off longing for the day that they could also dress in the short white dresses and white sandshoes. Both girls having the ideal, long legs for these clothes gained many admiring glances from the local males, young and old.

It was in the early stages of war that many quiet villages in England suddenly became invaded by our own British troops, forces camps sprang up in the most unlikely places and tranquil country lanes became congested with military traffic.

Young country people that were employed in reserve occupations had different views on this situation. Local young men in the farming communities rather resented the intrusion on their territory of all these dashing young fellows in uniform. The young ladies on the other hand rather enjoyed the extra male company that had suddenly joined them.

Newport was a village with a good selection of public houses, which drew many of the soldiers and airmen stationed in the surrounding camps. Actually getting to the village, which was several miles away from most of the camps did cause problems. Many of the young service men returning from leave took their bicycles from home back to camp with them. To see these young men going off duty on an evening was quite a spectacle, as they all made a dash to acquire a bike, any bike, to enable them to cycle to Newport and meet up with their new friends.

Many arguments occurred over the ownership of these bikes and good profits were made on the hire of them. Once a bike had been obtained it was a full time job keeping an eye on it while trying to enjoy oneself in the hostelries.

The local young men found this new competition more than irritating and would wait for an opportunity to steal the bikes whenever possible and throw them into the canal. When it came to closing time and the servicemen had to make their way back to their camps, after a good nights drinking, disputes would take place as they tried to distinguish any bikes that were still available.

As many of the lads didn't own the bike that they had arrived on, identifying them was virtually impossible and the good humour that had ensued all evening suddenly disappeared as tempers became frayed. Fights would break out as several people would try and mount a bike at the same time often resulting in at least two travelling on these poor machines back to camp, one stood up peddling, one sat on the seat and one sat on the handle bars.

Progress back to camp was slow and could be hazardous, to an onlooker the situation was quite hilarious, especially to the local young men! Those that were not lucky enough to have attained a bike would have a long walk back to camp, many of the soldiers and air men would have cycled from Tollingham and the delay in their return would obtain a serious reprimand.

Great changes were being made all over the country, families were moving from place to place as they had never done before. Families living in the cities, especially mothers and children moved into the country whenever possible either with relatives or friends so that they would be safe from the air raids, husbands joining them whenever possible. Housing in the country became limited as more and more families moved out of the cities, Mill House took its share of evacuees.

Chapter Sixteen

The War Effort

George had completed his training, Lily continued her work at home, Vera tackled her daily bike ride to Howden, Mable now prepared herself to leave school. Nora, the live wire in the family, arranged plays and concerts to raise money for the war effort and Bert was now at school, much to Lily's relief!

A great deal of knitting took place over the entire country during the war years, wool brought out of chests and cupboards that had been packed away for rainy days and when that ran out it was recycled from existing garments. Garments were knitted and sent to the troops, as all clothing was now only obtained through coupons according to availability.

Knitting took on a new look as people made do with whatever was at hand! Vera had purchased a pattern and wool to knit Nora a very chic little suit, not long after losing their mother when Nora was particularly low. The outfit consisted of a skirt, jumper and bolero all knitted in two shades of blue. Vera remembers Nora's impatience as the outfit took rather a long time to complete as it was knitted in fine wool on small needles. The effort was well worth the wait as Nora adored the finished garments and the pretty little girl did it great justice.

With George away, Lily and Vera having a hectic social life whenever possible Alfred felt the loss of Emily greatly, he handled his grief as best he could. It must have been very difficult for Alfred so soon after losing Emily seeing his growing girls suddenly very much in demand with these dashing young uniformed men. In the early months of the war when the wheels of bureaucracy were first set into motion it was decided that Lily and Vera would make excellent W.R.V.S. volunteers. Mr. Green, Vera's employer was usually in the midst of these decisions, he knew that the girls were intelligent and responsible.

Emily would again have been very proud. It was arranged that Lily and Vera would assist several of the more mature W.R.V.S. ladies with the evening meals that were to be provided for airmen that would be bussed out to the village each evening, and billeted in the village hall, out of dangers way that surrounded the nearby air fields. Lily and Vera were envied by other local girls as they would be in such close contact with the young airmen!

The atmosphere in the hall once these trainee pilots arrived was noisy and boisterous, Lily and Vera spent many very happy hours in the company of these clever characters. Vera was very quickly attracted to a pupil pilot whose home town was Isleworth, Surrey. He received his wings after only six weeks training and was then given leave, he returned home and wrote to Vera from there.

In his letters he spoke of a terrible, empty feeling that he had that just would not go away, after his leave he was posted to Oxfordshire for further training. Vera was shocked to have one of her letters returned, opened by censors but with no explanation. Vera wrote to his home and received a kind letter from his sister to say that Bert had crashed on a night training flight and sadly been killed. His sister arranged that flowers be placed on his grave from Vera. What a high price is paid in war, this was an extremely gentle, clean living young man of nineteen. As the war wore on they found it increasingly difficult to handle the fact that many of these young men went out on missions never to return.

It appeared that every possible pair of workable hands in Britain were working overtime! People worked hard and whenever they had the chance they played hard, walking miles to attend a dance or function whatever the weather. Newport village hall was no longer available for dances, this meant that the villagers had to travel to other nearby venues.

Hotham was one village that the girls travelled to, but was not one of their favourites as during the winter nights the only heating was from a coal or wood burning stove, supporting an upright chimney housed directly in the centre of the dance floor! As these functions were well attended space was always in short supply and the young women would find themselves fighting against their partners steerage as they neared the vicinity of the dreaded stove, many of them acquiring a burned bottom and ruined sooty dress. The bottom was easier to put to rights than the damaged dress, a precious commodity with the shortages of war.

Strict rules and regulations came quickly into force, such as food rationing and the black out. Rules and regulations are always unpopular with some and it wasn't long before a "black market," was formed in many areas, villages as well as in the cities. Where there is extra money to be made there are always unscrupulous people that will take advantage of the situation. It was because of this situation that Alfred was relieved that he had purchased his lorry when he did as he wanted no part of any under handed dealings. This is where many of the villagers would have surmised Alfred's finances for his lorry had come from.

Lily was glad of their well stocked vegetable garden, chickens for their eggs and the geese and ducks. Rabbits were always plentiful and made an excellent pie, it is sad to say that so did the pigeons that belonged to "Mill House!" Bert distinctly remembers time at school being spent digging the school gardens, and the head teacher's garden, at the adjoining school house. Vegetables were then grown, some to be used for the children's canteen. Bert enjoyed his days at school, his friends mother worked as a dinner lady at lunch time and always made sure Bert had a good helping and seconds if there were any to be had. He obviously hadn't read the poster, "A clean plate means a clear conscience. Don't take more than you can eat." Not that he ever left any!

Vera was kept busy with her work at the food office as well as the WRVS. Part of Vera's job was to issue ration books to everyone, they contained tokens enabling them to collect their entitlement of sugar, butter, meat and other general provisions as well as a sweet and clothes allowance.

Regular visitors to the food office were the local gypsies, who for some reason or another thought that they should be allowed more, Vera did not look forward to these confrontations.

Issuing permits for the slaughter of farm animals was another of Vera's duties and this was not always appreciated by the farmers, especially Alfred who didn't think that they should be told when they could kill their own stock. Vera spent many a troubled night worrying whether her father would comply with the rules as her job could well be at stake if he didn't, apart from the fact that it was a criminal offence.

At the office Vera made a particular friend of a girl a little older than herself called Dorothy. Dorothy was from a well to do local family of printers and even though Dorothy was engaged to be married she and

Vera spent a great deal of time together playing tennis or discussing Dorothy's forthcoming wedding.

Mabel excitedly looks forward to leaving school, she has been offered a job helping one of the local farmers wives in the house and as the situation stood at the time Mabel was happy to oblige. Mill House was a hub of activity at all times of day and night. Alfred stepped out of his bedroom in a morning and immediately felt he had walked into Hull Paragon train station, so hectic was the atmosphere with bustling adults and children. Lily constantly calling the younger ones to hurry or be late for school, Vera dashing about looking for misplaced items that were no longer in the safe place that she had left them the previous evening. Mabel happily going at her own pace as usual, Nora and Bert whisking in and out between peoples legs when they realise the time. When Alfred bumped into the lodgers from the front room, who were now virtual strangers to him, he sighed in despair, what has happened to his home. There was even talk of people bringing caravans to the country to escape the bombings in the cities.

Chapter Seventeen

The Summer

1940 - Alfred could hardly believe his eyes, there stood two caravans in his very own yard. Events took place so rapidly he had little recollection of any arrangements being made. I still find it so hard to envisage my grandfather in that environment, he appreciated his own space, even where his own family were concerned.

The city of Hull had taken a pounding with the constant night raids on the docks and local air aerodromes. Vera was relieved that she no longer had to travel into the city and would have been shocked if she had seen the devastation.

It still seemed unreal that situations could change so rapidly, only twelve months ago Vera had had a few days holiday with her lovely aunt Kate and uncle Jack. While staying with them her cousin Jack had suggested that they all have a trip to Bridlington on the East Coast for a day out in his recently acquired car. They made an early start, meeting some of Jacks' friends from his art college days for lunch.

Their spirits had been high, the weather great, the whole experience enjoyable. Jacks' friends were a jovial bunch, they had arrived on motor bikes or in an assortment of motor cars or vans! Vera wondered what would be in store for these gifted young people now. Jack was in a reserve occupation as he worked in art and design at a company called Metal Box in Hull. In later years he became a director of another Hull based company called Humbrol, who manufactured paints.

Most of the coast line of Britain was strewn with barbed wire, large concrete look-out posts decorated the beaches and cliffs, not that it mattered, no-one had time to worry about the picturesque locations any more, people were relieved to be alive. No-one had thought that this war would last, now things didn't look so optimistic. Families that had thought it would soon be over had made no plans to move to safer areas, now people began to rethink their situations. Many city folk found it extremely hard to adjust to village life, and many found it a totally different world, a world they unexpectedly liked even in the grips of war.

The latest residents to the Mill House property were the occupants of the two caravans parked in the yard next to the base of the old mill. When first purchasing Mill House one of its biggest attributes to Alfred had been the open yards surrounding the main house. Now everywhere looked cramped and untidy, it was as if the travelling fair people had moved permanently into Alfred's space, and there wasn't a great deal he could do about it.

The occupants may as well have come from a different world as far as Alfred was concerned. Both vans belonged to seafaring folk, something that Alfred knew nothing about. One of the couples were in their mid thirties and the other couple were slightly older, all from the city of Hull. The majority of the time there would only be the women and a couple of children in occupation, the men joining them whenever possible.

Mill House had become quite a little commune, a very lively commune. How my grandfather would have hated that word!

There were two families now living in the house with Alfred and his children and two families in the yard in their caravans. My younger aunts and uncles remember these war years with many happy memories, of the camaraderie and humour that goes hand in hand with trouble and uncertainty.

Sea faring folk have always been associated with liking a drink or two, or three! After many weeks at sea in terrible conditions, sailors and fishermen returned to their families and celebrated the fact that they had made their journey home safely. These people were no different and on the return of their men folk celebrations would begin! There was a general shortage of all drink as well as everything else in England during the war years but these sea faring people seemed to have an unending supply of goods of all descriptions from somewhere.

Alfred had never been a heavy drinking man but found it hard to refuse the kind offers of his tenants to join them in their celebrations, the outcome being that Alfred would become much the worse for wear and would have to be assisted across the yard home.

With George being away from home and the girls being in charge of the locking up of Mill House Alfred would on occasions find himself in an uncomfortable heap and locked out on his own door step in the early hours of the morning. He would then take himself round to the stables and join Blossom for another couple of hours sleep. Nothing would be mentioned the following morning at breakfast! The girls did not approve of Alfred's drinking.

Alfred was very strict with his girls and they had a constant battle as to when and where they could go. Earlier in the year Vera had been recommended to assist the newly formed L.D.V. (local defence volunteers in the area). The L.D.V.'s name was later changed to the

Home Guard. Another feat that Emily would have been most proud of as there were no other female Home Guards in the East Riding of Yorkshire. It was only because Vera was already in the W.R.V.S. that it was decided that rules could be bent slightly and Vera would do all the administration for this group. Minutes of meetings, keep records of all volunteers and their equipment, also accompanying Lt. Mills on his inspection visits.

Most of the Home Guard officers had gained their rank in the first World War, now being exempt from serving in the regular forces because of their age. These elderly gentlemen put their experience to good use in organising the public in the defence of their own homes and districts.

The Home Guard meetings would be attended by Lt. Ferrens,(one of the main streets in the city of Hull is named after the Ferrens family) Lt. Bellamy, Major Oughtred and Captain Saltmarshe. Captain Saltmarshe's estate was very near to Vera's home at Newport. An extremely quiet man, verging on being a recluse, Vera grew very fond of this elderly gentleman and over the next few years assisted him with private secretarial work at his home at Saltmarshe Hall, a beautiful Regency building on the banks of the river Ouse, the well kept lawns sweeping down to the banks of the river.

The Hall nestled among small farming communities on the lowlands at the edge of the Vale of York. Winding country lanes lead you through high gates into the park land of the Hall, where through the trees you would first glimpse the fine main building and majestic gardens. Captain Saltmarshe lived at the Hall alone except for a little help. Sadly he had never married and had no time for any of his distant relatives, he spent his time researching and writing. He told Vera on several occasions there would be a book about fishing that they would have to sort out when things became more settled. He spent most of his time at the Hall in one room only, he didn't believe in wasting money on heating or refurbishing any of the splendid rooms.

The meetings of the Home Guard were held in the upper rooms of the Wesleyan Methodist Chapel in Newport. Events took place regularly to raise funds for their area, very often in the form of a raffle. At one raffle Vera remembers a piglet being one of the prizes, Lt.Ferrens name was drawn out of the hat, causing great merriment. He immediately returned the ticket and because Vera was the only female there asked her to pick the next ticket. No-one was more shocked or embarrassed than Vera when it was her own name that she picked out. Vera made to return the ticket and the raffle be drawn yet again, but no-one would hear of it. Most I am sure thought this was an easy solution for a home for the little pig. Alfred would be most pleased with the addition in his pig sty, yet another worry for Vera as to Alfreds reaction for the extra slaughter permit he would have to obtain. No doubt Alfred would argue that a raffle prize didn't count!

On one occasion when all the Home Guards in the area were summoned to attend a documentary film held at the picture house in South Cave it was arranged that Lt.Ferrens would give Vera a lift. At short notice he was unable to do this and arranged that Captain Saltmarshe pick Vera up and drive her to South Cave. It had been arranged that they would all meet in the local "Bear Inn," before attending the film. The Inn as usual was noisy, smoky and packed to suffocation with loud banter being bounded about from the service men and locals.

Everyone made the most of their leisure time and would spend it in good company whenever possible, these local drinking houses provided a good and varied choice, whatever their mood maybe at that particular time.

Captain Saltmarshe and Vera enjoyed a drink with the others and they then made their way to the picture house to view their documentary. On entering, Captain Saltmarshe gestured Vera straight down to the very front seats, which had they been paying would have been the cheapest, many of the party found it extremely hard to suppress their smiles! Captain Saltmarshe would be forever frugal!

All events were made to be special, life in war time can be very short. The young people looking out at all times for reason to celebrate, seeming to harness a special energy to make the most of living, laughing and loving.

Chapter Eighteen

Uninvited Guests

The evacuees on the whole soon became integrated with the locals, everyone pulling together. There are, of course, some that will do more of their share of the pulling than others! One of Alfred's tenants, when her husband was away, would spend more of her time in the local public house than most. This young woman had two young children that she would leave unattended in "Mill House," this greatly offended one of the other women guests who would march down the road and insist on the return of the, by then, rather merry young mother.

Mill House had always been an open house for local people, particularly while Alfred was absent! Lily was a good listener, the kitchen regularly had unexpected visitors smoking and sharing a cup of precious rationed tea while Lily continued to do her work. One regular visitor to the house was a young man that one can only say was a little slow on the uptake, he enjoyed the company and usually jovial atmosphere that the house held.

My mother and her sisters remember one particular Christmas early on in the war when the girls where discussing their hair and clothes preparations for the coming events and in fun they suggested that they curl this young man's hair with their curling tongs. He, of course, enjoyed the attention even though at times the tongs got rather too hot and rather too near his scalp, he in fact was pleased with the end result, the girls thought differently!

It was now well into the second year of the war and very much in evidence even in the country. The Army practised building Bailey bridges over rivers, searchlights played across the night skies at the first signs of an air raid. Troops travelled up and down previously little used country lanes, in trucks, military cars or on motorbikes. The river Humber was watched over by huge barrage balloons, protecting the airfields and the docks.

The pupil pilots were no longer sleeping in the village hall, or not supposed to be, one of Veras admirers took it upon himself to stay over as it was far easier than returning to the lodging house that he had been allocated. His landlady reported him and he was severely reprimanded, as if they didn't have enough excitement! Lily had been good friends with a gentle giant of a Scots man, he was also a pupil pilot known to every one as "Jock". Lily was terribly upset when unexpectedly "Jock," just seemed to disappear off the face of the earth, no-one knowing his whereabouts. This became the norm, as over several weeks the student pilots faces became familiar and then just as quickly were no longer to be found. The girls automatically took this in their stride and befriended other young men in need of companionship.

Vera remembers travelling to Ely to visit one of her friend's families after he completed his training. Travelling during the war was not made easy as no station platforms had name plates and of course when it became dark there were no lights. This young friend of Veras called Les was to meet Vera at the station but for some reason they missed each other. Les, of course, was concerned after asking the ticket collector if a ticket from Doncaster had been handed in, it hadn't!

Vera had slipped through without giving in her ticket, luckily Les continued to look for her, eventually spotting her looking a little fraught! Vera had a wonderful weekend with this young man's family who made her most welcome.

On her return journey there was an air raid warning, which meant that the train connection that she should have caught at Doncaster did not arrive. Everyone was in the same position, conversations were soon underway among fellow travellers as to how to handle these inconvenient interruptions in their lives. Vera decided to spend that night in an all night cafe adjacent to the station, a long night of tea drinking and people watching was ahead. Early the next morning Vera was able to catch the first train home. Unexpected occurrences became normal everyday life during the war and people just muddled through, as long as their nearest and dearest were safe that was all that mattered.

Chapter Nineteen

A Perfect Day

After months of preparation Veras college and friends wedding day had arrived, a beautiful bright sunny day. Every minute of the day had been planned down to the last minute detail. No expense had been spared, Dorothy's wedding would be as special as any before or after the war. Every effort had been made by relatives and friends to attain the unattainable for the wedding party. It had been arranged that Vera would go to Dorothy's home and then be escorted by Dorothy's brother and his fiancé by taxi to the Wesleyan Church in Howden.

Vera knew very few of Dorothy's family and hadn't met the brother but found him just as she had expected, an extremely charming young man who had been at Cambridge University until just before the war. All the family being strong Methodists were none drinkers, Vera was quite taken back when on the drive to the church the driver was instructed to pull over outside one of the local public houses. Here she was quickly manoeuvred into the establishment and before she knew what was happening found a drink in her hand. Vera found the young couple most pleasant but had eventually to remind her escorts of the wedding about to take place!

Another colourful guest at the wedding was Dorothy's grandfather, other family members had been most interested in the arrival of this grandparent. He had Vera later learnt been married four times already, each ex wife taking a considerable amount of money when divorced. It was of great concern to the family that he may have another future bride by his side, they all breathed a sigh of relief when he had not! The family wealth had depleted greatly already.

As the church organ played the "Wedding march" and the congregation turned to see the bride being escorted by her father down the isle Vera felt a lump in her throat, an emotion that she had not been prepared for. Would she ever fall truly in love, dare she fall in love in these uncertain times, to commit to one person forever. Another emotion struck her like a bolt, her beloved mother would never see her marry, if she ever did.

Her moroseness was soon overcome as Dorothy caught her eye, her happiness was so apparent. Vera had already had the privilege of seeing the wedding dress, it had been laboriously hand made, exquisite in every detail. Tea-rose in colour, very heavy lace covering a satin lining, tiny covered buttons decorated the sleeves and bodice and the fit was perfect. The whole day was perfect, all the planning had paid off. Vera had thoroughly enjoyed the day but it was at events such as this that she missed her mother so much.

Regardless of the war, family life was family life, with all its ups and downs. There was plenty of both at "Mill House." Alfred still felt that he had his own private battle going on with his four girls, even Nora the youngest appeared to Alfred to be party to the female resistance group that was working undercover at Mill House, against him. There wasn't a great deal of conversation between Alfred and his three youngest daughters, Lily was the one that he felt most comfortable with. He was in fact most protective of Lily, whether this had anything to do with depending on her so much no-one will ever know. Lily was the one that he would question as to where she was going, who with, for how long etc. Lily didn't resent this interrogation and took it in her stride as she did every thing else, neither did she lie, she would just be a little evasive!

The two eldest sisters had hectic lives, Lily with her home commitments and the WRVS, Vera with her job, the WRVS and the Home Guards. Youth, thank heavens seems to give one endless energy, the hours the girls spent as their main occupation plus the extra voluntary work that they did meant that they would regularly burn the candle at both ends if they were to have any private social life at all. In the social life that they did lead the sisters were inseparable. Luckily the family were healthy and most of the time happy. Alfred would often catch the tail ends of conversations between the girls and after one of these occasions decided that he ought to pull the reins in on them a little.

One Friday evening Lily and Vera were making their timely exit when Alfred appeared from nowhere and enquired as to where they may be going in their finery. Totally honestly the girls replied that they were walking with friends to a dance to be held at the nearby village of South Cave, a good walk. Alfred's response was that they most certainly were not. The girls were furious and a battle of wills ensued for all of two minutes! They knew that if Alfred said no, he meant no. They also knew better than to defy him, but both girls were also strong willed and as Alfred stormed off the look they gave each other confirmed that they would not be totally beaten. They would do as their father wished and not go to the dance, but they would still go to South Cave with a slight change of venue.

Lily and Vera, light hearted again, proceeded with their walk, vehicles occupied with forces personnel and other young people waving and pipping their horns at them as they passed. Their spirits dipped slightly as they made a detour away from the dance hall and towards their aunt and uncle's home.

They were given a warm welcome as usual by their relatives, had a drink and exchanged family news before setting off on their return walk home. By now everywhere was blanketed in darkness, there were of course no street lights even if there hadn't been a war going on. The girls had their torch but that was to be used sparingly as batteries were difficult to obtain.

Well out of the village on the open country road, which was quite wide, Lily and Vera were aware of a dark silhouette of a figure approaching. It was obvious that he was not aware of them but the girls had no doubt that it was their father, going to check to see if they had disobeyed him and gone to the dance. It would be another night that Alfred would spend with Blossom in the stables as the two younger sisters would get out of bed to let the girls in and then relock the door. Alfred's time could well not have been totally wasted, as the older girls suspected that he had a lady friend somewhere in the area. What a different life all these young people would have lived had there not been a war, many would have lived. They would have had normal healthy lives instead of having theirs cut short before their time.

Those in reserved occupations who stayed in their own areas would never have had the chance to meet so many different people from other parts of the country and even world. They would have left school and most likely gone into an occupation that their parents and grandparents before them had done, marrying early, often to another local person that they had gone to school with. How the war had changed things, villages all over the country had forces from many parts of the world, America, Canada, New Zealand and Australia.

Life was certainly interesting and also frightening at times. The sisters knew fear, fear that the lively young men that they befriended

80

would not return from night missions. Many of the young pilots, friends that they had made did not survive, their loved ones would never get over their loss.

The war seemed to go on and on, Alfred prayed for peace in the world and peace at Mill House. George had had several moves from his first posting in Ayr, to West Hartlepool on Tyne and Wear followed by Dunbar in Scotland and later to Melton Mowbray in Leicestershire.

It was while stationed in Melton Mowbray and returning from leave that George became lost during a blackout in Leicester, he tried to make his way to the station but became totally disorientated. He decided to ask two young women that were approaching him directions, they struck up a conversation and George discovered that the two were working for the war communications in Leicester but came from Melton Mowbray where he was stationed. The girls walked to the station with him and he bought them all tea. George felt an immediate attraction to the girl called Kath.

Kath commented that she was returning home for the weekend as her brother was getting married and that George would be most welcome if he wished to attend, he gracefully accepted. A very pleasant and unexpected turn up for the books, George went back to camp a very happy chap!

Just over a year later on July 11th, 1942 George and Kath were married in Melton Mowbray, the only family of Georges that was able to attend was Lily, who travelled down by train. The rest of the families thoughts were very much with him. Kath was already lodging in Leicester so it was decided that the best plan was for this arrangement to continue and George spend as much time with Kath as the war would allow them. As it happened it was only a short time before George went over to France.

Chapter Twenty

A Long War

Memories faded as to what it had been like before the war started. Mothers grew used to their husbands, sons and daughters being called away. Friendships were formed as people tried to help other peoples families cope with separations, as they themselves were doing. Bonds were made that lasted many, many years after the war finished. Couples married maybe quicker than they would have done before the war, there was the constant feeling of urgency that went with uncertainty.

There was still a never ending stream of young pupil pilots being lodged in the areas around Newport. So many, devastating, if you really thought about it, better not to think at all. They acted as normal young people whenever possible, making the most of the weather, the hospitality and free time.

Lily was now twenty one and had been extremely touched when a married friend had arranged a party for her knowing that Alfred would not allow one at Mill House. At this time Lily had a friend that could play the guitar beautifully and together with Vera and her male friend they would ask permission to take uncle George's boat out onto his pond at the rear of his property. They did this with some secrecy, trying as best they could to avoid Bert and Sam (double trouble).

The island in the middle of the pond made a wonderful oasis of peace and tranquillity, if their plan worked. The willow trees, the warm wind on the water and the soothing music of the guitar playing their favourite tune of the time, "The people who live on the hill," somehow wasn't the same with cobbles whistling past your ears, coming from the direction of the bank. Bert and Sam thought this was wonderful sport, his elder sisters would no doubt get even with him at the first opportunity.

Bert was usually where he wasn't supposed to be. Another of his favourite pastimes was waiting for one of the occupants of the caravans to have a visitor, while her husband was away! Bert had worked out when this was most likely to be and would arrange for Sam or another pal to be there. They would squeeze quietly between the turnip house wall and the caravan, hardly being able to breathe. A window was always left open at this end of the van and as it was the kitchen end there was usually an assortment of goodies within reach. Goodies that many families rarely saw during a war, so not only did they have some enlightening entertainment they also had free refreshments!

Mabel no longer worked for the Brown family, much to their disappointment. She had been told of a vacant position in one of the retail wholesalers in Hull called Millers owned by a Jewish family. After giving it much thought Mabel had applied and to her surprise was accepted and given a position on the drapery department. The lady in charge of this department was married but went by her maiden name of Pashley. Miss Pashley immediately warmed to this quiet, placid, friendly girl. This lady and her husband sadly were childless, along came Mabel who was so easy to love, almost instantly a very special friendship was formed. Mabels life changed as quickly as Veras had when she had first gone to college, travelling to the city each day, new friends to be made and most of all the feeling of independence.

Emily had a cousin that lived in the Spring Bank area of Hull where the Millers warehouse was situated and as soon as they heard that Mabel was working so near to them it was arranged that she should have her lunch with them each day.

It was also arranged that Mabel would spend so many nights at Miss Pashley's home on the outskirts of the city to save her the travelling and the expense. A great fuss was made of Mabel in both these homes, luckily she was not the type of girl to take advantage and gave as much happiness as she was given.

Nora now feeling very left behind by her older sisters could not wait for the day that she herself would leave school. There was a great deal of disruption with children's schooling at this time, the growing of vegetables had become virtually as important as the three R's. Luckily Nora was a bright child and a willing scholar with never a shortage of friends. The three older sisters all agreed that Nora being slightly smaller in stature resembled their aunt Kate more than any of them, she also had the same sunny nature which added to her natural prettiness.

As the age difference appeared wider at this particular period of time, Nora hardly yet a teenager and Mabel now feeling almost worldly with her new job and added freedom Nora found companionship with a young girl called Doreen Harrison. They would spend hours together riding their bikes, getting made up if they could lay their hands on the older girls precious make up and generally pretending that they were five or so years older! Even the children had their part to play in the war years and many schools organised the collections of empty glass bottles, jars and any other useful commodity. They were called The Children's Salvage Corps.

84

One fine summer's day in the school holidays Nora and Doreen set off on their bikes with a picnic for their lunch to visit aunt Mabel in South Cave. On their return journey Nora skidded on a bad road surface and was thrown off her bike, she fell heavily onto the ground and became unconscious for several seconds. Nora's friend was distraught and thought that she had died, when they finally returned home Nora was checked for concussion but it was her friend that went into shock.

Another friend of Nora's was called Valerie Freer. Valerie's father arranged for villager's Sunday papers to be delivered to their homes and a job of delivering was offered to Nora, and Valerie. The area that Nora covered included Broomfleet and her grandparents home. The papers had to be delivered in all weathers and as it was a lengthy bike ride in bad weather it would take Nora most of the rest of her Sunday to either warm up or dry out. The five shillings that she earned and the free dinner kept Nora going.

Bert changed little, still as full of mischief as ever. It looked as if he would be an eternal Peter Pan. A Peter Pan with extra adornment of colourful cuts and bruises often topped with a good layer of mud or dirt, even the odd plaster cast! Lily had the patience of a saint. Sam, Bert's friend lived a few doors away from Bert's cousin Maurice. He was three years younger than the two friends and would dearly loved to have been in their company, Aunt Ethel was having none of it. George and Ethel were extremely strict and protective with Maurice after losing their daughter Brenda.

Chapter Twenty-one

Company

1942 - Europe was still being ravaged by war, food shortages became more apparent. In the light of day life looked grim, peoples' only escape was into a fantasy world created in the ability to transport oneself into a different world, either with the help of music, alcohol, crazy company or a very special loved one. Some went for the full package!

The public houses and dance halls were always full, those on leave needed good memories to get them through their next tour of duty. Lily and Vera frequented several different drinking venues in the area, depending where their friends would be. Occasionally they would make the journey to Brough on the bus, this journey was only made if the person was rather special! In the spring of 1942 they were continually asked by two Military Police officers to visit the tennis courts at Brough and play a game of doubles with them. These two M. P.'s were quite a lot older than the girls, and married, but they were good company and they were very proud to be seen with these two attractive young women. Needless to say that game of doubles did not materialise.

The Albion in North Cave was one hostelry that was extremely popular with the army and the airforce, it was while here one early autumn evening that Vera suddenly felt eyes upon her. Looking up she saw a strange face watching her, not strange peculiar but strange as unknown.

Immediately she felt unusually self conscious, she was aware all evening of the young man's interest. As the publican rang the bell to call the last orders before closing time the young soldier approached Vera and asked if she and her friends had far to travel home. From there the time went so quickly, they only had eyes for each other, as they say. Before they knew where they were they had been manoeuvred out onto the street. Roy, had introduced himself and was desperately trying to make a date to see Vera again, it was arranged that they would meet at the White Horse pub in Gilberdyke, which was only a couple of miles from Veras home. This was later to become their regular meeting place and Mrs. Foster the landlady would let them light a fire and go into the front room.

Roy must have been keen as it was a return journey on foot of approximately nine miles from his army camp at North Cave. Surprisingly after their first date the couple became an item, surprisingly because Vera had found Roy rather too amorous and had told him quite plainly he had to behave himself or the friendship would be over before it had begun!

As the days grew shorter and the weather colder spirits dropped. How long would the war prevail, how much of a pounding could Britain take. We gave back as good as we received and more. Soldiers on the front line staying strong for their families and their families staying strong for the troops.

Christmas approached and every one made an effort, especially for the children. There was little to be bought in the shops and no

Christmas feeling in the city streets, as there were no brightly lit shop windows because of the blackouts.

Regardless of the situation in the country, in general, Vera had not been so happy for a long time. This quiet, dark and unassuming young man from Staffordshire had altered Veras life completely. Comments had been made pointedly to Vera that it was unusual for her to date anyone other than an officer, Roy was a corporal! The attraction was quite obvious when unexpectedly Roy called at Veras office while he was on his inspection round of the search lights, the other young women were most impressed.

Roy made his inspections of the search light batteries accompanied by a long time friend called Wilf Powner also from the Potteries. Being members of the Territorial Army they had received their call up papers at the same time. There was one problem, Roy had claimed that he was sixteen years old to gain entry to the territorials when in fact he was only fifteen. The reserve forces are always called to serve their country before civilians. Roy's mother had not been pleased, Roy was the eldest of her three sons and she idolised him. He was also a great help to her as his father was a deputy pit manager and worked long hours with a great deal of responsibility.

Wheels were set in motion and by the time all the paper work and other legalities were put into place Roy just scraped in with his age. Wilf promising Agnes, Roy's mother that he would take great care of her son. A friendship was formed that would last all their lives. Roy had first applied with Wilf and several of the other territorials in their regiment to join the Staffordshire Yoemanry, this would have involved light armoured cars.

They were told that this regiment was full and it was suggested they join the Royal Engineers. The R.E's suited Roy as at the time he was serving an apprenticeship as an electrician. Roy's regiment was based in Northampton and it was whilst here that it quickly became apparent to Roy's superiors that when working with electronics he stood apart from the crowd. From Northampton he was referred to Nottingham University for several months training in electrical magnetism. Roy later rejoined his regiment but regularly gaining more knowledge attending further courses in the subject.

The one thing that Roy did not enjoy about attending many of the courses was that he would be billeted with a civilian family. He much preferred to be with the lads. He didn't feel comfortable in a stranger's home, whereas most of his comrades preferred it. Roy had also been brought up with very high standards and some of the lodgings would not have been classed as five star!

Quite unexpectedly Roy was called before his commanding officer and offered a position of an instructor to officers, he was still only a very young man and to leave the rest of his pals and have to daily mix with his superiors, Roy found a daunting thought. He agreed to do a trial period at the end of which he would be allowed to return to his unit if he preferred. At the end of several weeks Roy decided to do just that, everyone had been most pleasant and it was obvious that Roy was more than capable to do the job. Sadly he was spending so much time with the officers that he now felt that he had become an outsider to his own ranks. Roy had many attributes but ambition was not one of them. Vera was to realise this many times in the future, Roy is still a kind and caring people person, these characteristics do not usually go hand in hand with ambition, more than fifty years on Vera wouldn't change him for the world.

Chapter Twenty-two

The End Is In Sight

Another spring, another summer, George had been part of the D day landings in France in June 1943. He drove a Bren gun carrier to the docks at Tilbury and then loaded it onto the waiting ship, the troops then assaulted the French beaches in landing craft. It was here that George's regiment, the infantry, joined forces with Canadian troops and they drove their gun carriers, following the coast line into Holland. There were six men to a gun, every river or canal had to be crossed on a pontoon bridge. George remembers many of his comrades feeling more sea sick on these bridges than actually being in the middle of the Ocean! It was to be over two years before George returned to England.

There were now more shortages than ever, people knew they could no longer make further cut-backs on food and provisions. Vera heard this every day in her job at the Food Office where the ever reliable posters cried out their messages of advice, "Food is a munition of war, don't waste it!." There were worries of nutrition deficiencies for young and old. One item that wasn't rationed was compassion and this was a time when the British were not too shy to openly show their feelings, regardless of the stiff upper lip!

Women were taking on more training to assist with previous male dominated jobs. The woman's Auxiliary Territorial Service took over more of the driving when ever possible. Roy remembers the post being taken over by the W.A.T.S, suddenly the regiment appeared to receive less post than usual. It wasn't until the post vehicle went for a service and the floor mats were removed that the reason became apparent. A good deal of mail had not reached it's destination, feathers flew!

The W.R.V.S. also widened it's scope for the war effort, my mother remembers being trained in morse code and having to attend shooting practice that was held in the grounds of the brick works. The thought of my mother with a gun I am told caused a great deal of laughter, she could not focus a camera in the right direction never mind the barrel of a gun.

It was when Roy's regiment was transferred to the East Riding of Yorkshire to maintain the search light batteries that he had met Vera. It wasn't long before Roy became a regular visitor to Mill House, Alfred instinctively realising that this young man was not one of Vera's general platonic friends. Alfred made no comments, which wasn't unusual! The only time the girls remember him doing so was at a time he had heard that Mabel was keeping company with a young French Canadian airman. Alfred made it quite clear that this member of the allied forces would not be welcome at Mill House, obviously there had to be a connection with Alfred's time spent in Canada amongst the French Canadians.

Roy was no different to anyone else and felt a magnetism to Mill House and its occupants, there was never a dull moment from entering the ever open gates to the drive. Bert was very often the first to encounter, telling some sort of tale usually about one or another of his sisters.

The young male visitors were warned well in advance, apart from the fact that they had done exactly the same sort of things only a very short time ago and they enjoyed the banter that would take place with Bert and his shadow, Sam. It was the near to normal family life that most of the visitors enjoyed, as it was the disruption of the war that had caused families unforeseen separations and it was this that most families found so hard to bear.

During the spring and summer months a team to play rounders or cricket in the paddock was always readily available. Ages ranging from the very young to very elderly, there was no age discrimination. Stray chickens and the pony would make a hasty retreat, their adjoining neighbour Dr. McKenzie would give them a cheery wave but decline to partake.

Several rows of cottages backed onto the paddock at one side and it was quite usual to become a rather heated affair as teams formed either into family groups, males verses females or civvies verses forces. Competitiveness ran high and a return match promised on the close of the game. Roy became quite envied in his billet, not only did he have a good looking, local girl friend but she had three very good looking sisters.

The life at Mill House was worlds apart from Roy's own home life, one could only say that "Manyana," was a word that sprang to mind when thinking of Mill House! Roy's own mother was an extremely organised person who had to have every thing in its place.

Chapter Twenty-three

Family Meeting

It was in the summer of 1943 that Roy arranged to travel to Stafford-shire with Vera to meet his parents and two younger brothers, Eddie and Bill. Vera was rather anxious and Roy rather excited about the coming event. Vera anxiety grew as they approached Roy's family home, that his parents owned. Both their parents were very much in the minority in the fact that they owned their own property, as at that time home ownership was not the norm. In fact, it was only in the early sixties that the British public began to purchase their own homes.

Vera's first impressions of the large semi-detached house was of an overall neatness. The long drive and perfectly manicured garden, the pristine paint work and general well kept appearance. When the front door opened she was warmly greeted by a rather surprisingly short lady, as neat as her property, with very black hair and the most beautiful blue-violet eyes.

Vera was instantly aware that her worries had been unfounded, Roy's mother Agnes immediately took to this trim young woman that Roy had chosen to bring home. Vera was surprised that Agnes did not have a strong Staffordshire accent, Agnes had also expected Vera to support a stronger Yorkshire tongue. Both women were softly spoken and refined. Roy's father Fred would not be home until he had finished his shift at the mine.

Eddie, their middle son had been devastated when he had been turned down for the forces because of a perforated eardrum, he had wanted to join the Royal Marines. He was definitely the charmer of the boys and dressed exceptionally well taking a lot of rude remarks from his brothers. He was serving his apprenticeship as a joiner and drove his mother crazy as he had to have an early start in a morning to travel to his job, she dreaded every morning, threatening to leave him in bed and let his father sort him out on his return.

Eddie would have fitted well into a different life style, on one occasion Frederick and Agnes arrived home after a couple of days away to find Eddie had a horse tethered on Frederick's precious lawn, Eddie was learning to ride and had the full riding outfit. As a small child I thought he was a film star, his dress, his cars and his overall quiet manor oozed charm.

Bill was the youngest of the boys and having recently left school was working at a local butchers. Customers began to frequent the shop for the entertainment as well as the quality of its meat!

While Agnes made them tea Vera was able to take in her surroundings and very impressive they were too. This wasn't a comfortable, well worn, country cottage or an ordinary family home there was an extra something that Vera could not place, she was later to learn that Agnes had been a colour matcher for a pottery company. An extremely gifted talent that could not be learnt, you either had the natural talent or you didn't. Agnes had been brought up by her wealthy aunt and uncle as her mother had died after the birth of her brother when she herself was three. Agnes knew from personal experience that however good people were no one could take the place of your own mother. It didn't take long for Agnes to realise just how much Vera still missed her mother and her heart went out to her.

Agnes' home reflected her expertise in colour co-ordination and the standard of comfort that she had been used to. The uncle that brought Agnes up took the place of her father and she took his name of Marsh. He had a well established painting and decorating business, holding the contracts for schools, hospitals etc. Because of his artistic flare he also advised the decor for many of the very wealthy Master potters properties.

Agnes's own family, the Bloor's, had in fact owned Crown Derby during the middle and late 19th century and during that time brought chinaware down in price so as to be more accessible for the general public. Being born and brought up in Staffordshire there were many opportunities for young people's artistic talents to be brought to the fore. Agnes had uncles who were china painters, one in particular was George Bell who for a time was employed by Minton.

Agnes's flare for colour may well have been nurtured by the gentleman she called her father, she had a great deal of love and respect for him, as did her three boys.

Vera found Roy's family home most relaxing. Relaxing until the entrance of William, Roy's youngest brother known as Bill. During Agnes's last pregnancy she had been desperately wishing for a daughter, it was not to be and when their third child was born he was named John William, he was irresistible. Every one loved this happy cheeky little chap, until he became two or three years old and then quite naturally he and his older brother, Charles Edwin - "Eddy" didn't see eye to eye over anything. The sibling rivalry caused Agnes a great deal of worry and it had very often been Roy who had defused situations. All the family missed him a great deal while he was away.

Bill reminded Vera so very much of her own younger brother Bert, always so full of fun, and so loud.

Vera found the open adoration that Bill had for his older brother Roy extremely touching, also the closeness of Roy and his father whom Vera found to be a gentle man. Vera left Staffordshire with Roy feeling part of his family, which had overcome a hurdle in itself, as Vera was a very private person.

Chapter Twenty-four

Lily's Surprise

Another winter and still in the grips of war. George still in France or Holland, somewhere in Europe. Lily battling with cleaning, cooking, washing and all the other daily household chores. Vera cycling to and from work in all weathers, helping Lily with unfinished jobs that had to be done before they could go to their W.R.V.S. jobs or to meet their friends.

Vera would still accompany Lily when Roy was on duty and unable to see her and Lily would very often meet up with friends of her own when Roy joined them. The two sisters remained the closest of friends regardless of Vera's relationship with Roy. Mabel was still working in the city, staying over several nights a week to save her travelling. Nora had now left school and was doing very well working in Brough, travelling each day by bus. Bert had grown very tall but had changed very little in any other way!

Christmas had come and gone, people had made an effort but it had been a huge effort. It became increasingly hard to keep warm and feed a family. Even the rabbits that had once over run the fields had become scarce.

Vera remembers returning home on those cold dark nights of January and February feeling lethargic after the long ride home, hoping that Roy would suggest meeting her near to home. All she wanted to do on those cold bleak nights was to curl up in front of their bright log fire, Roy had spent many hours assisting Alfred in the sawing of the logs on his frequent visits to see Vera. It was a job that none of the other male visitors to Mill House volunteered for as Alfred was a hard taskmaster and would complain that his partner tending the opposite end of the saw was pushing not pulling! Which apparently affected the rhythm of the sawing.

On Vera's return home from work Lily would be ready for an evening out. With great enthusiasm, and knowledge, as to where their crowd would be and how they could get there. Vera felt guilty as Lily spent so many hours at Mill House, it was obvious she needed to get away for a break a few evenings a week.

Vera's energy returned with the Spring, she felt herself again, looking forward to the future, whatever that may bring. Roy and Vera had discussed getting married, no further plans had been made. No-one knew what tomorrow would bring, Roy could be sent to Europe at any time. Vera had touched briefly on the subject with Lily but she had got little response, she had felt quite hurt at first but then thought how Lily would feel her loss if she moved away. The two girls had always been inseparable, more so after the loss of their mother. They saw little of Mabel when she was at home now as she had met a young man in the R.A.F. he was in the ground staff based at Tollingham, his name was Chris and he was from Sheffield in the West Riding of Yorkshire. Mabel had met him at a dance, he was full of fun and they made a perfect couple.

Lily, Vera realised had changed, she no longer wanted to go out, it took a great deal of persuasion to get her to go anywhere. There had been other things that Vera had thought odd, had she imagined it, that conversation between her other sisters and their close friends had suddenly come to a halt with her appearance?

Vera had passed it off at first, her and Roy had been spending more time alone, that would be it. Over the next few weeks things didn't get better as Vera had hoped they would, they got worse. Lily became more distant with Vera, Vera tried several different ways of asking her what was troubling her. Nothing did any good until one night when they were getting ready for bed Vera told Lily how the distance she was putting between them was upsetting her. It was then that Lily dropped the bombshell, she was five months pregnant! Nothing could have prepared Vera for this, she reacted more as a mother than a sister. How could she have done this, how could she have been so stupid, what would their father say, what would everyone say! Lily hit on this remark, everyone knew Vera would be more bothered about what people would say, she was well known as the family snob!

Vera's main concern regardless of what others thought was what would happen to Lily's future now? The other sisters had known for several weeks, so had one of Lily's friends. Time and time again, Vera asked Lily why oh why hadn't she told her earlier? Who was the father of this child, had Vera met him, did Lily know his regiment? Vera got as much out of Lily as she could, now she would have to swallow her pride and ask for help.

Luckily the officers that Vera mixed with in the Home Guards had a certain amount of influence. Vera's old friend again came to the rescue advising her of who to get in touch with and where. Vera felt almost responsible for Lily, why hadn't she noticed, how could she not have known. Lily must have felt terribly alone, this was why she had been so desperate to go out in such terrible bad weather earlier in the year. Lily had hoped to see the young man that she had become good friends with. Then as often had happened before with out any prior warning the young officer had been posted.

It was because the young man was an officer that Vera was told that there was no way that they could divulge any information on his whereabouts or personal details. Vera, Roy and their close friends continued to make their own enquiries but they led them nowhere.

Time went on, the baby was due in early September. Lily and Vera started to realise just how little they knew about the facts of life. One of the couples that had lived in Mill House at the beginning of the war still kept in touch with Lily and they arranged to visit her. The lady was a good few years older than Lily and Vera and was certainly more worldly, she managed to reassure them that they would cope as many other young women were having to. She was just sad that it had happened to someone like Lily, although she knew she would make a natural mother.

Chapter Twenty-five

An Unexpected Proposal

There were no longer any of the evacuees living in Mill House by now. When it had become apparent that the war was to go on longer than expected the guests realised other options would have to be found. Living in cramped conditions was all very well for short periods but not long term.

The two younger sisters were becoming quite excited about the coming event, Vera was still in shock. Their father had to be told, this was a task that Lily had to do herself. Alfred made little comment and the subject was not discussed again. How they all missed Emily. Bert wished people would tell him what was going on.

There were still more shocks to come, Roy's regimental posting came through to go into Europe at the end of June that year. His regiment was first based at Brighton, while there Roy and a soldier were sent on a delivery to the Woolwich Arsenal. When they returned their regiment had gone! They had been left a note to join them at an American camp in Southampton, Roy remembers the rations were excellent, he would!

They then found that there were going to be delays in their crossing into France, they were told any soldier wanting to get married could have a weeks leave!

A good number of personnel decided it maybe a good idea after all including Roy. He remembers it being like a rugby scrum, every one wanting to use the public telephones. People leaving messages with near strangers to warn of their unexpected leave, relying on their proposals being accepted!

Vera received this unexpected call whilst at work and her colleagues wondered whatever was the matter, such was the shock on her face. Vera didn't know if she could handle it at this moment in time, she had spent the last few months constantly ringing around and writing letters on Lily's behalf. There was so much to do, a special licence to obtain, the bans, vicar and church to organise. Apart from the things no man would think of such as a dress, flowers, cake etc. All the time Lily was on Vera's mind, how could she marry at such a time when Lily would feel more alone. When Vera came off the telephone her head was reeling, she sat down and her friend Dorothy joined her, waiting for Vera to speak. This was just the sort of venture that Dorothy thrived upon and when told of the day Roy would be arriving back in Yorkshire realised that there was no time to spare.

Enquiries began that very minute. Roy was to ring Vera later the following day to see if it had been possible for their wedding to go ahead the following week. Rev. Bottomley, the Newport vicar arranged all the paper work for Vera with the vicar at the Howden Minster for the wedding to go ahead at their local church in Newport. It was decided to keep the proceedings low key partly because of Lily's situation. Details were finalised, Roy rang his parents who, of course, sent their blessings and good wishes.

There was a great deal of sadness as they would not attend the wedding, it was arranged that Vera and Roy would spend three nights in a hotel at Bridlington after the wedding and from there travel to Staffordshire.

Vera's colleagues at the Food Office threw themselves wholeheartedly into the wedding preparations. Dorothy arranged to take Vera to her own home for lunch the following day, to Vera's surprise Dorothy's beautiful heavy lace wedding dress lay draped over the couch. Very little food was eaten during their lunch break, the dress fitted like a glove and Vera was loathe to take it off. The matching headdress and veil completed the ensemble perfectly. A bouquet of Tea Rose roses was ordered, also button holes for the groom, best man and Alfred. One of Vera's colleagues and her husband had on occasions accompanied Vera and Roy to functions and it was arranged that her husband Leslie Jackson would be Roy's best man. Within the space of only a couple of days a wedding had been organised!

Friends were wonderful, rallying round to help where they could. One of the local grocers, Ethel Cox, provided Vera with just enough dried fruit for her to make a small wedding cake, all the staff at the Food Office donated items of food for the buffet that was to be held at Mill House. They also received some very unexpected presents, particularly as it was war time. The officers from the Home Guards presented them with a grand dressing table brush and comb set, purchased from Carmichaels, a jewellers in the City of Hull. The telegrams of good wishes from the Ferrens brothers and Capt. Saltmarshe I have to this day.

On the beautiful summers day of 12th July 1944 Vera proudly became Mrs. Frederick Roy Allen. Roy returned to Southampton, with a number of newly married solders!

He vividly remembers waiting to board the ships, that they called Liberty ships. They patiently waited on the quay sides in an atmosphere he will never forget. American black cooks serving hot food while they waited. Roy landed on the beaches at Omaha, a code name given during the war, following an American de-embarkation. His regiment were then to spend the next fourteen months in France, Holland, Belgium and Germany. As every other old soldier he has many tales to tell.

Vera and Roy's Wedding Day 12th July 1944
Alfred & Les Jackson to the right

Chapter Twenty-six
The Next Generation

What a difference six months can make in a lifetime, who would have guessed within the year of 1944 Vera would become a married woman, Lily would be awaiting the birth of her baby and Mabel had found the love of her life. Nora was doing well in her new career and Bert and Sam had a new interest in life, girls. Heaven help the females of the East Riding! Very little mail was received from George who was in the thick of the action in Europe.

Mill House, still as active as a bee hive with adults, children, animals and vehicles coming and going at all times of the day and night. Lily was restless in the late stages of her pregnancy unable to sleep during the heat of the summer nights. Alfred returning home being prepared to be locked out, following seeking solace with one of his female friends. The summer fruits had been harvested and bottled or jammed, the apples would be the next and last fruit to prepare before the onset of winter. Lily's pregnancy had gone well, there was no shortage of food at Mill House and it was hoped that Lily's baby would be healthy and strong.

The girls had virtually carried on their lives as normal except for the fact that Lily seldom ventured outside the Mill House boundaries. This did by no means imply that Lily was short of company, quite the contrary she had so many visitors that no sooner had the house emptied of the family than they would appear again, requiring attention.

It was during the evening of the fourth of September that Lily confided in Vera of her experiencing the first signs of the oncoming birth. Both girls were in their twenties but extremely naive in such matters. How they wished that their mother was there to support them. Very little had been organised for the event which to the girls had seemed to be so far in the future. When it was quite obviously so imminent their common sense took over and a plan of action was made.

The younger members of the family would be kept unaware of the situation until Vera had contacted the local midwife and the situation accessed. Lily had a very uncomfortable night and Vera a very anxious one! On the fifth of September 1944 while the house was empty except for Lily, Vera and the midwife, a baby boy, Graham was born. Vera was with Lily throughout the birth but found the experience so traumatic that she has no recollection of it at all. Nevertheless Vera loved this baby boy as a son, as all the Leighton family did and still do.

There was great excitement on the return of the rest of the family. Bert was delighted, he felt he had a baby brother. Even Alfred took an interest, the baby was male after all! The four sisters rallied round and gave Lily as much support as possible but it was obvious that Lily was not going to need any lessons in bonding with her baby, her love was there for all to see.

To Alfred life must have seemed to have gone a full circle, Mill House with a baby again.

The family were relieved that Lily held no bitterness as all their searching for Graham's father had got them nowhere, Lily was forever the optimist. She gave so much love to others she deserved the love of the father of her child, this was not to be but this didn't harden Lily as it would have done to many others in her position.

Mill House now held more love and laughter than ever. Vera returned to work to find that all her colleagues had bought presents of clothes with their rations for Graham. Lily was very touched and grateful for their kindness. Alfred paid this small child more attention than he had ever given his own children and would very often be seen bouncing him up and down on his knee while singing the song "Danny Boy." From then on, Alfred was known as "Danny Boy" by most close family and friends.

Lily's pregnancy and the birth had all gone smoothly, Lily was feeding her baby herself until she developed an extremely painful breast abscess. This caused some anxiety for a while in case of an infection but after a short course of antibiotics they were relieved that their worries had been unfounded.

The progress of the war in Europe overtook everyone's lives in Britain, people constantly tuning into their radios for the latest news, even though this of course was censored. The radio would be run on an accumulator, a heavy block which would have to be taken to the local garage to be topped up, a spare was always kept for such occasions. All inconveniences that we do not have to experience today.

Lily now with the baby and Vera, a married lady, most evenings for the two elder girls would be spent at home, Vera only going out to Home Guards meetings, where Capt. Saltmarshe would still insist on calling her Miss Leighton!

Vera also tried to pursue Lily to accompany her to the W.R.V.S. but Lily would decline. Lily spent every spare minute she had with her baby, he grew more beautiful every day and at only a few months old he had a mass of thick blond curls and he could charm the birds out of the trees. At Mill House he was never short of an audience.

It was now Mabel and Nora that spent their weekends socialising at the dances, Alfred paying more attention to his new grandson than to the whereabouts of his two younger daughters. Vera would spend many an evening writing to Roy, longing for him to return safely home.

Chapter Twenty-seven

1945 Victory

Every one was relieved to feel spring in the air, it had been a long, cold hard winter, there was great hardship all over the country and all over Europe. The world was praying for peace. The residents of the Channel Isles, in particular, were having a hard time since being occupied by the Germans, many were starving and risking their lives daily working for the resistance movement.

It was the first week in May 1945 that the first good news broke, the British and allied forces regained the Channel Islands. This really lifted peoples' spirits and week by week we gained ground in Europe, until on June 6th Peace was declared! This brought mass euphoria here and right across Europe, the Second World War had been raging and destroying everything in its path for nearly six years.

One picture Roy would never be able to free his mind of was that of young children, as young as ten, that had been brought into Europe by the Germans as slave labour from their countries in the Eastern block Poland, Latvia and Rumania. Many were behaving like vicious animals and had at first to be restrained by the allied forces until they could gain their confidence, which obviously took time.

One of Roy's regiment failed to return after a night patrol, he was later found murdered, it was thought by a group of these extremely frightened children. The young man was known by his pals as Duke as he was always dressed just so, whatever situation they were in.

Most British people partied and partied until they no longer had the energy to party, which didn't take long as the last six years or so had sapped away a good deal of their strength. People celebrated the fact that their loved ones had survived, those that had lost their nearest and dearest rejoiced that there would be no more blood shed in Europe, the war in the Far East still unhappily continued.

Changes were taking place at great speed yet again, troops being brought back to England to go into reserve occupations, such as mining, building and engineering. Many of our cities would have to be totally rebuilt.

George had been fighting at the front and no-one would be more relieved to set his feet on British soil again. Kath was hoping for George's imminent return, but it wasn't actually until the following March that Kath would welcome him home.

Lily had little time to indulge in thinking of much else other than the normal routine at Mill House but on the rare occasion it did enter her mind as to what lay in the future for her and her wonderful young man, now growing so quickly.

Vera also wondered what lay ahead, young people at that time didn't plan too far into the future, not when they had been going into war. Her and Roy would have a great deal to discuss.

Mabel and Chris had already made plans to marry, hopefully they could now set a date for the near future. Nora was still working at the aerodrome in Brough. Bert although not old enough to be leaving school had plans of his own, he was adamant that he would become a mechanic. He would be found with his head under the bonnet of his father's lorry tinkering with things that were not broken!

October 1945. Roy had been de-mobbed from an arsenal in Woolwich and placed in a reserve occupation as an electrician in the mines in Staffordshire. He did not tell Vera for many years that his superior officers had tried to persuade him to stay in the army as a regular, his skills would still have been highly rated even in peace time. Roy was no different to most young men, all he wanted was to return home to his new wife and family. The returning soldiers were easily recognisable in their ministry issued suits and Trilby hats. Vera recalls the young men going into the Food Office to collect their ration books, Mr Green (ex military man) the officer in charge would make a big issue of asking them to parade their suits and hats, most participating proudly. Spirits ran high so soon after the conclusion of the war.

Only a few weeks before Roy's demob his younger brother Eddie had married a local Staffordshire girl, also called Vera. Sadly, Roy and Vera were unable to attend the wedding, life was still hectic as people tried to put their lives back together. Roy made two purchases with his demob money and his rations, one was a heather coloured Harris tweed overcoat and the second was an old Standard Eight car. Most newly married men were saving for household items, not Roy!

The Food Office became busier than ever as people returned to their homes and information on their ration books had to be brought up to date. Vera remembers Gracie Fields (famous Singer) sister, Betty, visiting their office. Gracie had spent most of the war years in the USA taking Betty's two young children with her. Betty had married a well known comedian called Dougie Wakefield from Gilberdyke. Dougie had a row of cottages built in the village for his mother to rent, George bought one of these many years later and still lives there today.

It was decided that Vera would remain at Mill House for the time being and continue with her job while Roy accessed his job in the mine. He had no intention of remaining there any longer than necessary. Their time together was very precious as Roy worked long hours making it difficult to travel to Yorkshire as often as they would have liked.

Roy's father had retired early from the mines and had decided to move to the west coast, Blackpool, to make a living, putting his assets into property.

Alfred had also decided to sell his coal business. When this became general knowledge he was approached by a local Gilberdyke gentleman called George Terry. A deal was made and Mr. Terry took over the business which he ran for nearly forty years.

It was twenty years on now from Emily and Alfred purchasing Mill House, Emily had seen thirteen of them. In some ways the actual house had stepped in and become part of the stability and strength that had gone with Emily, all families need to belong and Mill House was their safe sanctuary. Alfred would now spend more time on his own property and working when needed at farmer Kirk's.

Lily had her hands full, not only with Graham who was now a sturdy little chap, but with Bert, now nearly fourteen. He and his partner in crime, Sam, would still be in the middle of any mischief that there was to be had in the village.

The local dances in the village hall had started up again after the premises had outlived their use as an out of camp base for the young pilots. The toilets to the recreation hall were outside earth toilets. At the rear of the ladies toilet block ran a narrow open vent approx. a foot from the ground, Sam and Bert would find long, strong stinging nettles and insert them into these vents in an upward direction on hearing some unsuspecting young woman approaching. Hence one badly nettled bottom! They managed to go undetected for some time but after being threatened with a good hiding from some of the older local males decided to give up and find a new venture.

The village hall was also used for political meetings, Bert would encourage his father to attend knowing that his father's temper would get very heated and he would have to be restrained from a fight. Bert would take bets on the outcome from his friends!

While the Labour party were in power and tax was increased on tobacco Alfred swore that he would never smoke another cigarette and give his money to the Labour party and he didn't, little did he know what a favour they had done him.

Chapter Twenty-eight

A New Start

Vera had discovered that she was pregnant prior to Christmas 1945. There were many difficulties to be overcome for the newly de-mobbed, newly married, young people in Britain. Housing shortages were one of the main problems, many people starting their married lives living with family or friends. Roy had been living with an aunt and uncle in Stoke-On-Trent as his parents had moved to Blackpool, this arrangement would not be suitable when their baby arrived. Mabel and Chris had arranged their wedding for October that year, Mabel was then to move into Chris's family home in Thurgoland, near Sheffield, West Yorkshire.

Nora was hoping to have an interview and be able to replace Vera in her job at the Food Office when Vera joined Roy in Staffordshire. There was a need for rationing for several years after the war.

At the Home Guard meetings Capt. Saltmarshe still insisted on calling Vera "Miss Leighton" even when several months pregnant! It was arranged that Vera and Roy would live with Roy's old army friend

Wilf and his family in Stoke-On-Trent, Vera was to move there a couple of months before their baby was due.

It was a sad day when Vera left the Food Office, she and her colleagues had gone through a lot together. Her friends at the office had become Vera's second family and now they were happy to welcome Nora. There was a bright new future to look forward to, a couple of years earlier people had started to doubt it may ever happen. After what Europe had gone through they could face anything.

Leaving the office had been hard enough for Vera but leaving Mill House and Lily was going to be harder. The two girls were going to miss each other greatly. Leaving Graham was also going to be difficult he was such a loveable, little chap now eighteen months old and running everywhere. As in all good sized families there are times when there is so much happening that keeping track of one's own actions is difficult, this period was one of those times.

George had come home and he and Kath had moved into the Mill House flat, George had decided to start a haulage business using Alfred's lorry that was now redundant. Mabel was in the throws of her wedding plans for October, Nora was happy in her new position at the Food Office and Bert had been offered a job as an apprentice at the local garage. A few weeks before Vera's baby was due Kath announced that she was pregnant.

The Leighton's contribution to the British Baby Boom!

In March 1946 Vera joined Roy at the home of his friends Wilf and Jess Powner in Stoke-On-Trent. Jess was a few years Vera's senior, with two children already in the house to look after Jess appreciated any help Vera gave her. The two women were as different as chalk and cheese, a very similar relationship that Vera and Lily had shared.

Jess putting off anything that could wait until tomorrow whereas Vera would prefer to get things done and sorted. The relationship worked well, Vera more than happy to spend a good deal of time neatly ironing while Jess noisily put the world to rights! The arrangement suited both couples, Jess becoming a substitute mother to Vera as her confinement drew nearer.

In the early hours of Wednesday, the ninth of May 1946, Vera realised that their baby would shortly be born, she said nothing to Roy as he left the house for work. Roy returned home to find he had a baby daughter, he was delighted. Only a short while after receiving the good news Roy enquired if Vera could get up to do his tea!

Earlier while discussing the event Roy had made it obvious that he would prefer their baby to be a girl, it had been both their preferences. Roy's mother who had so desperately wanted a daughter now had a granddaughter, she couldn't have been more pleased.

Several names had been considered, Emily after Vera's mother, Leslie after their best man at their wedding and Susan, at the time a popular name. Susan it was to be as both parents also liked the abbreviated version, Sue.

Roy, Vera and their daughter spent several months with Jess and Wilf, during which time Roy's mother and father decided to move back to Staffordshire. Their new granddaughter may have had some influence in their decision!

Only a few weeks after Roy's parents moved back to the Potteries, Roy and Vera joined them in their new home. Bill had moved with them to Blackpool but had missed his pals and was pleased to return home, he hadn't planned on there being a baby in the house though and he was a little apprehensive. He turned out to be much more adaptable than he had imagined and found this little niece most entertaining. He also realised the joy that she had brought his mother and knew that in the future he and Sue would be great pals.

It was arranged that Lily and her friend Elsie would travel to Stoke by train for Susan's christening. It would give Lily a welcome break from routine, Mabel and Nora would look after Graham while they were away. It may have been after the visit from her sister that Vera became a little homesick, she loved Roy so very much but she also missed her family. Mabel's wedding was also to take place in a few weeks time. Roy was not settled in the mines and letters from Yorkshire told of many job opportunities.

In the late autumn Vera and Roy returned to Yorkshire with their baby, Roy being released from the mines only because Alfred had the small holding for him to work on.

Chapter Twenty-nine

Back Home

Back to Mill House! The family fold, just in time for Mabels wedding on the twelfth of October 1946, Hull Fair week! Vera felt that Mill House held her arms out to embrace them. All the family together at last, this was going to be a special wedding. Kath had offered Mabel the use of her wedding dress and veil which was very much appreciated as clothes were still on ration. Chris's relatives were to travel from Stocksbridge and return the same day, his two young nieces were Mabels only bridesmaids. It was a bright autumn day and as at all happy family events there was great jollity and camaraderie. Emily would have been so proud of this family of hers.

Graham now two years old, was at first intrigued with the new baby in the house but became less interested daily as he realised she didn't do anything other than eat, sleep and get bathed. Alfred showed no interest in her whatsoever. Vera found it strange at first without Mabel. During the war she had spent several nights away from home each week but this time it was different. The door would open and close and on several occasions Vera expected to look up and see

Mabel's smiling face. None of the sisters knew when they could expect her home again. Mabel wasn't finding her new home, shared with Chris's mother, an easy task, his mother had suffered with her nerves for several years and on occasions was difficult to deal with. There was no-one more patient than Mabel, Chris's cousins and other relations gave her a great deal of much needed support.

George and Kath were now settled in the Mill House flat but George's plans for the haulage business were not progressing as he had hoped. Existing local firms were making things difficult for George to get business, resulting in him becoming very down hearted.

Some of these other businesses had done well in the black market and as this was no longer needed there became rivalry amongst new business and the boys that had been at home during the war. George told Kath little of his concerns, constantly teasing her of the coming event. He had returned home in the March of that year and their baby was due in the November! He would want to know what had been going on if this baby arrived earlier! He didn't, Jeffrey was born on the eighth of December 1946. There were now three babies under three years old at Mill House. All the sisters thanked heaven for all the long washing lines and good drying areas just as their mother had done before them.

Roy had been told of vacancies at a company called Capper Pass only a few weeks after returning to Newport. He decided to call in person and present himself rather than write a letter. He travelled on the local bus as the factory was situated on the main route to Hull. He left the bus and followed the instructions he had been given.

Two factories stood relatively close to each other, as he approached he noticed the well tended gardens and pavilion. He followed the signs to the offices and while doing so a small gentleman emerged from one of the buildings. Roy asked this chap if he could tell him where he could find the chief engineer, as luck would have it Roy was speaking to him. He asked Roy what experience he had, Roy must have made a good impression as the engineer asked him when he could start. It was only on leaving the open gates, and reading, what had previously been out of sight that the factory was not Capper Pass but Earls Cement! Roy had alighted the bus at the wrong stop, what good fortune, as he was later to find out that Capper Pass was not the healthiest company to work for.

Chapter Thirty

More Moves

The Christmas of 1946, what a happy affair. Mill House ringing with the sound of children and adults merry making, the wonderful aromas of Christmas spices from puddings and pies. Nora rushing off here, there and everywhere socialising, she is still the same today over fifty years on! Bert and Sam cruising the village looking over the local opposite sex.

Bert had at that time started his apprenticeship as a mechanic but would at a later date have to do his National Service. Most young men were called up at eighteen unless they were doing an apprenticeship when the call up age was then twenty-one.

The years that followed had all the usual family ups and downs, thankfully more ups than downs. Just before Sue's first birthday Roy and Vera moved from Mill House to a village called Melton, this is where Roy was employed at Earls Cement. It was a company house that they would rent. There was one drawback, the house was still occupied by a long term tenant, an elderly gentleman that had been employed by the company for many years. The gentleman was called Mr. Hatfield, and I (Sue) called him Granddad Hatfield.

Sharing homes at that time was quite usual practice, after having the evacuees at home Vera hardly noticed. I can remember the old gentleman riding me up and down on his foot and singing, "Ride a cock horse." I also remember him being cross with me for treading on his strawberries when going to the bottom of the garden to meet my daddy from work. My mother would take me shopping to the next village, Welton where my great aunt Mabel had been in service. A pretty village, circling the church, green and pond. A brook ran from the pond and I remember paddling along in my wellington boots after doing the shopping.

Sweets were still on rations and one of the local shop owners would give me currants and sultanas as a treat. These memories are very vivid along with many others, even though I couldn't have been any older than three.

Vera and Roy lived in Melton for a couple of years and were then offered a flat in Hessle. The company had bought the old nunnery that Vera had passed many times as a girl on the way to their picnics at "Little Switzerland." The company had made an excellent job of converting the old building into good sized, well equipped homes. Vera and Roy jumped at the opportunity of such a home. There were twelve flats in all, allocating them proved to be difficult, everyone wanting this, that and the other! It was eventually decided to put each apartment number on a piece of paper in a hat and each person in turn draw one out. The number drawn being their new home. Roy was delighted with his luck, it was the number Roy would have chosen, number seven, Dykes House.

Their new home was on the first floor, at the front of the building with a spacious lounge with french windows opening out onto an elaborate ironwork balcony and wonderful views of the river Humber. On a clear day the Lincolnshire countryside on the opposite river bank could be seen. The balcony also overlooked the sweeping terraced lawns flanked by stone steps and large urns, huge cherry trees acted as a divider prior to the vegetable gardens. At the bottom of the garden was a gate which led onto the road along the river. Across this road was another gate set into a high hedged paddock belonging to Dykes House, this led straight onto the foreshore.

Bert hadn't been working long before he met the young girl that he would marry, Anne, a striking red head that had joined the office staff at the garage where he was employed.

They would visit us in Hessle, they took me on the river path to learn to ride my bike. I remember falling off, their minds must have been elsewhere! I also remember them at Mill House on the usual Sunday family gatherings when Bert was on leave while doing his national service in the R.A.F. Anne always sat on his knee, something I found very strange at the time. As far as I could see there were plenty of vacant chairs!

Alfred had purchased a Hillman car by this time, Bert commandeering it for the majority of the time. It proved to be most useful for his courting! Part of Alfred's routine was a weekly drive to a large market in the town of Selby, approx sixteen miles away. Alfred was not known for his good driving as the years wore on and the rest of the family would only accompany him if someone else drove. Mabel remembers on one outing Alfred buying a bicycle and Bert riding it home, meaning Alfred would have to drive the car on the return journey.

Mabel said many prayers on that homeward drive, spending the whole trip with her eyes tightly shut! Lily would wait anxiously for their return, never knowing what Alfred was to purchase. Their cupboards were full of china tea sets and linen, he could never resist a bargain. Nora did have a few driving lessons, but her father and brother may not have been the best of instructors at the time.

By now Nora had moved offices into Goole where she met a young man, he was rather dashing I always thought! She met him the day before her twenty-first birthday, what an excellent present. His name was Ted Retburg and he had been a Paratrooper, his father was Danish hence their surname. My early memories of Nora and Ted is of them in their finery, getting ready to go dancing. There was also a period of Nora knitting, not something that lasted long. The garment had to be knitted on huge needles in deep colours, very fashionable at the time. I used to ask her to save them for me when I grew up. At that time every thing appeared very glamorous in my eyes, the colours, the perfumes and preparations before an evening out. The young males in uniform, no longer with the look of apprehension that they must have worn during the war years, now replaced with happy thoughts of a good future.

Roy had now been in his job over two years, he worked a long day and very often Saturdays and Sundays, nevertheless he was very happy in his work and earning a good wage. They were also comfortable in their new home, the apartment was heated by radiators which were operated from the basement and heated the whole building. Very few homes at this time had such luxury.

There were a number of children in the building which meant that I had plenty of company. Vera had made a couple of friends and was kept busy with general home making but missed her job in the office atmosphere a great deal. Maybe in the future she would return to work.

My parents and myself remember these years as most happy ones, there were a number of real characters amongst our neighbours which enriches life. I recall the smell of fresh baking bread, children sat talking on the stairs in bad weather, rolling down the steep banks of lawn in fine weather and the heavily laden blossom of the cherry trees.

Standing under the blossom when it started to fall while it showered all around you, making dens in the evergreen shrubbery, heaven for children. On summer evenings after getting ready for bed being allowed to watch the yellow painted boats glide up the Humber loaded with butter, while standing out on the balcony in the warm night air, very often perfumed from the garden flowers beneath.

Another strong memory is of the coronation party held at Dykes House to celebrate the crowning of Queen Elizabeth in 1952. We were able to watch the ceremony on the television and later enjoy a huge spread of goodies set up on large trestle tables in the entrance hall, patriotically decorated in our red, white and blue.

Chapter Thirty-one

Child's Play

Regular visits were made to Mill House by my mother and I, usually on a Tuesday. We would walk along the pleasant tree lined avenues to Heads Lane to catch the bus, the journey taking an hour or so. I remember trotting along enthusiastically on the way there but having a struggle to stay awake on the return journey, those beautiful, huge old trees looked very different and threatening when the nights grew dark.

Our visits were never quite the same when Graham started school, I missed him terribly. Jeff was still at home but he was always a very quiet little boy. He is a slightly shorter build than Graham and myself, because of this plus the fact that I classed myself as much older, I remember wanting to mother him with his cheeky grin and wonderful curly hair that I was very envious of!

I would be allowed to stay at Mill House for a few days during the school holidays, very unsure of my mother returning to Hessle without me at first, but soon settling into helping my lovely aunt Lily and pestering Graham. Eggs had to be collected from the stables and hen houses and then washed ready for the Egg Marketing Board to collect.

Vegetables had to be picked from the vegetable garden for dinner and when the time was right raspberries had to be collected for customers or Lily's home baking. Spring was as always a magical time with fluffy chicks and other baby animals. Piglets were my favourite and whenever possible I would persuade my aunt to let me put one in an old dolls pram and push it around the yard. My grandfather's response would be a grunt, he was obviously as pleased as the sow! If a piglet wasn't available the next best substitute would be a kitten, there were usually a number around.

It was the geese that I was afraid of, I wouldn't dare cross the yard to visit my aunt Kath in case of being attacked by these vicious birds. When it came to bedtime I would sleep with my cousin and my aunt. Very often, Graham and I would still be awake as Lily and Nora made their way up to bed. We would have been playing "I spy," even in the dark. Graham would tell me to hold on to the bed or his mother's weight as she got into bed would catapult me out.

Lily was still trim but I would believe him and we would both suppress giggles as she approached the bedroom. The next thing I would know was waking to the cock crowing, and the sun shining. Is it happy memories that we associate with bright sunny days? I remember few rainy days at Mill House.

As I grew older I made friends with the local girls. One particular lasting friendship still very dear to me today was with a local farmer's daughter, Beris Underwood. Mill House as ever would always be a place for young and old to stop and have a chat.

There seemed to be so many things to do, the old chest in my grandfather's bedroom full of children's books, boxes of lead soldiers and farm animals. Outside rope swings hung from beams in the stables and ladders to explore the hayloft. Our grandfather still had his sporran from his Black Watch uniform. We were not allowed to play with this or other items of our grandfathers but we did!

Graham would wear the sporran and Alfred's funeral bowler hat, high leather riding boots and play (or pretend) to play a banjo, heavens knows where the banjo came from but we certainly enjoyed our dressing up games. By this time the old lorry was no longer in use, it became our favourite pastime. Aunt Lily would cook us chips at lunchtime and we would all pile into the lorry to eat them, travelling the world in our imaginations. There was a period when the flat bed of the lorry had a hard top placed upon it. The only access into the back was then to climb through a tiny window above the passenger seat in the cab. This I found a great struggle as I was well rounded at the time, the fear of being stuck half way through was quite unnerving but I was determined not to be left out of the games whatever the consequences!

During the school holidays the farmers would have surplus milk, as less quantity was required due to the schools being closed. Every child had a small bottle of free milk each day to help keep them healthy. Obviously this unwanted milk wasn't good for the farmers economy but was a great treat to me, milk straight from farmer Kirks cows. I would listen for the rumble of the trolley wheels that would indicate that my grandfather was approaching pulling a churn containing the wonderful rich liquid. Even as a small child I knew that I would have to ration myself, or be terribly sick! The same went for many other delicacies while staying at Mill House. Helping make the sausages after the killing of a pig was another enjoyable but messy pastime.

Show days were particularly memorable, relatives that rarely visited because of family or work commitments would be warmly welcomed, Uncle Fred amongst them!

Fred hadn't changed over the years and had been in trouble for assault on his local vicar, in all fairness to Fred though the vicar had been having an affair with Fred's wife! He was a loveable rogue and no-one could be cross with him for long. As he got older he developed sugar diabetes and had to spend long spells in the hospital. The ward staff must have dreaded him being admitted as he could cause havoc anywhere, even in hospital. Some of the patients became regulars with these complaints, therefore making friends.

During one of his long spells in hospital he and one of the other patients lay awake until everyone else slept and the ward sister had gone for her break, they then tied several of the beds together by the legs. In the early hours of the morning when the occupants were rousing Fred and his pal gave the ropes a huge tug sending several beds whizzing across the ward. I have yet to hear of anyone else being expelled from a hospital!

Chapter Thirty-two

Family Wedding

The weddings that took place also brought the family together, they happened at regular intervals for a number of years, as did the births of their children. Nora and Ted married at Newport in October 1954, I was extremely excited to be one of their two bridesmaids on the occasion, dressed in a long pink, water-marked taffeta dress.

They later had two children, David born in February 1957 and Sandra in 1959. This was all very exciting to me and on occasions I would go to stay with them in Goole where Nora and Ted had their home. David had the blondest curly hair and Sandra had very dark straight hair, both beautiful looking and good natured children.

On 14th July 1956 Bert and Anne were married at North Cave. This time I wore a pale blue lace bridesmaid's dress. Their children, two boys Nigel and Paul followed in 1958 and 1960. More babies for me to mother, Nigel often supporting rather a worried look for a small child gave me every excuse to give him lots of attention. Paul was a very different character, much more confident as a baby.

There was a worrying time when the family thought that he was maybe deaf as he made no attempt to speak long after he should have been saying at least a few words. After several hearing tests it was apparent that there were no hearing problems. The fact was that he wasn't going to make the effort to speak when his elder brother understood his needs and accommodated him them!

Mabel and Chris sadly had no children of their own but in 1959 did adopt a little boy of six called Stewart. Stewart could not have chosen a better Mum and Dad anywhere.

Family times at Mill House were wonderful. On occasions meals would be in two sittings, with the children eating first. Our uncle Chris was a terrible tease and I would do anything so as not to have to sit next to him at the table, if it would accommodate us all. By this time there were eight children, which seems an awful lot when you are an only child and if all the adults were present there would be another twelve mouths to feed.

In the summer months the usual game of rounders would be played in the paddock.

Even as adults all the siblings knew what tasks were needed of them, Mabel and Nora would do any decorating necessary, helped by any male that they could pursuaded to give their time. My own mother, Vera would tackle any needlework in the form of mending. I remember watching her turning the collars on my grandfather's shirts with such tiny neat stitches. It wasn't until years later that I realised how she hated sowing and what a tedious task this must have been for her.

Their cousin Maurice met a local girl from Sandholme called Carol and when they married I was a bridesmaid yet again. The old saying, "Always a bridesmaid never the bride," did cross my mind on several occasions!

Chapter Thirty-three

Returning To Work

In 1953 it was decided that Vera and Roy along with Roy's parents would buy a large semi-detached property in a prestigious area in Hessle and convert the property into two apartments. This house called Derry Lodge was in the leafy lanes of Southfield. The sale went ahead and the conversion was first class.

My grandparents were to have the basement and ground floor and my parents the first floor and attics. What an adventure, for an eight year old. I believe the property had been used for evacuees during the war years and had been terribly neglected. The garden resembled a jungle which suited my grandfather totally, overgrown with large trees and shrubs.

After weeks of chopping down, pruning and general clearing a beautiful sunken Italian style garden was discovered complete with a summer house.

132

A long drive down the side of the property led to an old stable that was to be converted into a garage. There was already a resident in the old building, a majestic white barn owl. I would patiently wait for him to appear, in awe of his beauty.

Part of the plan for this move had been so that my mother could return to work and for a while this was successful. Sadly, my grandmother didn't settle in suburbia and after a couple of years it was decided to sell the property and my grandparents return yet again to Blackpool. My parents then had two subsequent moves in Hessle and in later years to North Ferriby followed by a return to home ground for my mother to Gilberdyke, North Cave and later, Laxton.

Vera later resumed her career in commerce and did very well, spending many years at Owbridges Cough Mixture a family owned business in Osborne Street Hull, leaving only when the business was taken over by a large drug company. Other interesting employment followed and Vera finally retired in her late fifties.

During the nineteen fifties Vera kept in touch with her aunt Kate and uncle Jack in Hessle, as we only lived a twenty minutes walk away. As they got older I would accompany her when she visited, taking baking or other requests. They appeared very old and tiny in my eyes at the time but I will always remember them as being kind and happy. Uncle Jack passed away and life became difficult for Kate, she had diabetes and through this had eventually to have both legs amputated. You never heard her complain, she continued to live alone with only the help of a cheerful little Welsh lady that came in each morning to get Kate ready for the day, returning in the evening to assist her to bed. Aunt Kate was one of the sweetest people I have ever known. I associate her with Lily of the Valley and peonies, flowers that seemed to flourish with abundance in her tiny back garden. My mother sadly missed her when she passed away.

Chapter Thirty-four

Family Holidays

The Leighton girls and their families continued to meet whenever they could, including holidaying together. When possible they would visit the north side of Blackpool, the quieter part of the coast, staying at Roy's parents or in nearby accommodation and meeting up during the day. Roy's parents would have been classed as property developers today as they would buy and renovate houses making a good income. None of the family remember visiting the same house twice! All were only a few minutes walk from the beach which was very much appreciated.

Lily didn't take part in these trips sadly, she would stay at Mill House with their father who by this time was of course ageing. Graham was always part of the group however, I looked upon him and looked up to him as my big brother. These times where particularly enjoyable to me as we would also meet my father's brothers and families, this meant that I had both my families around me.

Sadly my grandfather, Roy's father passed away in 1959, things of course are never quite the same. My grandmother stayed in Blackpool until she reached the age of eighty subsequently joining my parents in the East Riding of Yorkshire. Shortly after my grandfather's death Bill my father's youngest brother married, he always said he wouldn't marry until he was thirty, and he didn't! What a party animal, no-one thought it was possible for any one to tie him down. The girl that finally managed to was a local brunette called Delrae. Bill had certainly seen life, sailing on the Queen Mary to America and later travelling into Canada where he worked for several years. I would longingly await parcels from him containing unusual gifts, flimsy blouses and moccasin slippers were but two.

In later years Bill and Delrae adopted a son, Jonathan, who is only a couple of years older than our own son, making him feel as much Nick's cousin as my own, we share him!

Chapter Thirty-five

Modern Conveniences

There were very few changes at Mill House, the usual on going maintenance jobs that have to be carried out on any property plus the addition of electricity and modern plumbing conveniences, such as a bathroom and inside toilet.

By this time there was only Alfred, Lily and Graham living in the family home. Numerous visitors as always of course and even though there were less people for Lily to look after the house hadn't shrunk in size and there was just as much cleaning to be done.

However tired Lily must have been she was always the same, happy and smiling, willing to listen to anyone's troubles or worries. Never complaining herself. In the future years I would take over the job from Nora of home perming my aunts hair, which was wonderfully thick. When I had wound half of her head of hair on perming rollers I would think that the job would never come to an end as she had so much. When the perming process was finally finished I would look at my aunt and think what a good looking woman she was. The only reason that I could think of that she had never married was that she was perfectly happy as she was.

Many of Alfred's grandchildren were now at school, the eldest now at Comprehensive schools but because of the eleven year gap in the reproduction of the Leighton clan the younger group had not reached school age. Graham and Jeff both attended the comprehensive at Melton, called South Hunsley. Both boys being very bright found the work easy going. I wished I could have said the same, I found most work hard going! This didn't mean that I didn't enjoy many of the subjects because I did, especially art, history, geography and English (except for the spelling)!

The whole family were extremely proud when Graham became the head boy at his school. My own father had also been the head boy and later his brother's daughter Carol had the same honour. What acts to follow!

There was to be an addition to the younger group members of the Leighton children. Mabel and Chris were approached by the social services and asked if they would foster a young boy of eleven . It was arranged that this young man called Derek would spend some time with them to see if he settled, and if he and Stewart were compatible.

I recall first meeting him and immediately warming to the large eyed young boy who was so quiet and who was obviously weighing up the situation. This is now thirty six years ago and Derek is now as much a part of the family as anyone.

Chapter Thirty-six

Mr. Right

Time marched on, accompanied by the usual childhood ailments followed by teenage hormonal peaks and troughs. Turbulent first crushes and loves, all the things that life throws at you. Upheavals of house moves, job applications and one of the most important, meeting Mr or Mrs Right!

For some reason I always imagined marrying a farmer, but after accompanying Graham to several village dances I did have my doubts! Graham had two good friends, brothers of a local butcher that I was very fond of. When starting my first job in retailing, working for a well known Dutch company the three boys would pick me up and drive me into Hull on a Saturday morning. They worked on a butchers stall in the Hull market owned by the boys' father. That drive gave me a good start to those Saturdays, they were always so full of fun.

Mr Right came along for me on New Years Eve, 1963. My parents had by then moved to North Ferriby, I was celebrating the new year with friends at a local hotel called "The Duke of Cumberland". This young man and I travelled to work each morning into Hull on the train.

The young man was called Mike and by rights he should have caught the earlier train, as time went on he became a regular passenger on the later! We became inseparable and the following year began to make wedding plans to take place in 1965, if Mike passed his degree in chemistry.

Graham had also found his soul mate, Joan. Jeff was soon to follow with Ann.

Then came the whole procedure of family weddings yet again. My mother and I accompanied Lily into Hull to buy her outfit for Graham and Joan's wedding, which must have been quite an ordeal for her. By the end of the day I think she surprised herself by actually enjoying the occasion. When the day came and the Leighton clan collected at Mill House prior to going to the church, the whole family were delighted for Lily, she looked such a picture.

On this day in particular Lily must have wished that Graham's father could have shared in her immense feeling of pride. Still only a young woman, her beloved son was now leaving the nest. How I had wished some knight in shining armour would come and carry her away to cherish and protect her. Lovely kind Lily.

As coincidence would have it shortly after our wedding Mike was offered a good position at a chemical company in a market town called Selby where Alfred supported the Monday market. Graham's fiance was a local Selby girl, they decided to buy a house in the same village that we were living in and we virtually became neighbours, separated only by a field.

The years passed and eventually all except one of Alfred's and Emily's grandchildren married and settled in Yorkshire. Mabel and Chris's son,

Stuart, very sadly had a fatal road accident when he was twenty. It had been a cold November night with the first frost of the year.

In his new white Beetle car Stewart had lost control on the ice and his car left the road. No one else was involved. Happily he had lived life to the full, enjoying every minute of it. He was a good looking, clever chap who had just received the apprentice of the year award from his employers. At his funeral the church was full and mourners filled the church yard. I will never forget my aunt telling me that God had only lent him to them!

Derek and Stewart were both very different characters but over the years had grown very fond of each other. How hard it must have been for Derek to see his foster parents grieving, the family that he had become such a part of and found such stability with was suddenly missing a huge piece. Derek had by now joined the army, hearing the news of his brother's death he applied for compassionate leave, which was refused on the grounds that they were not blood brothers. How this must have added to his grief, would this cruel act still happen today?

Alfred became frail with age, suffering increasingly each winter with a bad chest. He refused to see the doctor and when in pain with ulcerated legs Nora would have the unenviable job of dressing them for him, with cows udder oil! That was the only preparation that he would use and it usually worked!

Eventually he became more tired and would only leave the house to walk round the stables. Mike and I by then had our son, Nick who in turn, with his partner, Claudia of course, gave us our wonderful granddaughter, you, Saskia. Without you I would have had no reason or inclination to put pen to paper, to tell you the story of your great, great grandparents in the East Riding of Yorkshire, England.

Nick enjoyed his visits to Mill House, but admits was a little afraid of the stern looking elderly gentleman, whose studded working boots clicked loudly on his entrance to the yard. I had loved my grandfather dearly but only in the last few months of his life did I feel that he acknowledged me at all, it was a wonderful feeling.

After a cold hard winter, after a last walk to the stables to see his beloved horse Alfred passed away peacefully in his bed, on 9th March 1973. He and Emily would be together at last after so many years apart

Chapter Thirty-seven

Changes For Lily

What changes lay ahead for Mill House and Lily now? Lily was at the family home alone. Finances had grown tighter over the last few years and it wasn't apparent to the family until looking into Alfreds affairs after his death that he had been given no financial advice from his bank whatsoever. If he had, his financial situation may well have been very different. There were many repairs that needed to be done to the property and Lily had no pension.

Many family discussions took place, many ending in disagreement. As always each individual family member came under scrutiny. Alfred was the kind of man that kept things very much to himself, not discussing the siblings private arrangements with him, if there were any. Everyone was in agreement without doubt that Lily should have the choice of either staying at Mill House or maybe buying a small bungalow in one of the villages in the area. There was one problem, the shortage of cash. The estate was worth a good deal of money but that would mean it would have to be sold to release any.

The outcome eventually was that Lily would go out to work and continue to live at Mill House, now a very empty house.

Lily found employment at the local aircraft factory in Brough, the largest employers in the area where during the war all the young pilots in the area had done their training. What an ordeal this must have been for her, now in her fifties, never having had a job in her life before.

Lily was to work in the packing department as she had no special skills. It meant that she would have to rise early to catch the local bus to travel to Brough, returning in the evenings the same way, in the winter months to a cold empty house.

George and Kath still living in the Mill House flat came to an arrangement that a fire would be lit for Lily's return each evening, which must have been a welcoming sight for her.

In her usual manner Lily handled the situation well, outwardly anyway. Not wanting to be a trouble to anyone, she just got on with the job in hand regardless of her inner turmoil.

This was a period in my life that I saw less of my Leighton family than I had previously. I had started a business of my own and had a young son and husband to look after.

After spending a weekend at my parents, on our return journey home we called at Mill House to invite my aunt to visit us the following weekend.

On entering the house we were totally shocked to find Lily very distressed, sat in the kitchen with Bert and a couple of friends. Lily was having pains in her chest when breathing and in general felt really ill. Over the next few weeks Lily had many tests and the conclusion sadly was that she had lung cancer, at quite a late stage.

The family were totally devastated. Lily had never smoked in her life, but had spent hour upon hour in the Mill House kitchen with numerous friends who smoked constantly.

After having surgery Lily returned to work for a short period and she did I believe enjoy some of the company, but she had been so used to her own pace in life that it must on the whole have been extremely strange and alien to her.

As Lily's condition grew worse the family took it in turn to nurse Lily in their own homes everyone wanting to do their best for her, as she had done for them. The last few weeks of Lily's life were spent in Sutton hospital in a suburb of Hull, as she became too ill to be nursed at home. In the short time that she spent in the hospital the nurses gained a great fondness for her quiet gentleness.

Somewhere out there in this wide world was a man that had missed so much, if he had lived through the war and was still alive. He had missed the love of this wonderful woman and also a fine son that he didn't know existed. What sad consequences, all because of a war! Lives where lost in more ways than one.

Lily died in 1978, at the age of fifty eight. What a sad day that was for the Leightons.

Mill House, so sad so empty, as if pleading with you on your entry to stay and bring things back as they had been in the passed. Suddenly everything and everywhere looked tired, worn out, even grim without the occupants that had shared its air and space for over fifty years.

Different avenues were taken, plans were drawn and passed by the council for Mill House to be bulldosed and a small estate of detached dwellings built which would bring in a substantial amount of money. Hard decisions were taken by the Leighton family, deciding against this course of action.

George and Kath's home was still in the Mill House flat, this must have been a most unsettling time for them waiting for the family's final decision. It was at this stage they found that Lily had already distributed certain items belonging to Alfred after his death, some of Alfreds war medals, the gold sovereign ring and other personal effects. This of course caused a certain amount of disharmony with the siblings.

Alfred had been a great hoarder, inside as well as out. Many of his aged farm tools were greatly appreciated at a museum in York. Any furniture requested by the family was given, other pieces not wanted were sold to an antique dealer. We all chose objects that held particular memories dear to us. The one thing that affected me more than any other was watching my cousin Sandra carefully pack the Cottage Ware china. Even though I knew that it was going to a good home where it would be cherished I felt my childhood days at Mill House were being packed away at the same time, gone to me forever.

In a relatively short period of time Mill House was put on to the market, a buyer found, a price agreed. As easy as that, gone!!

As coincidence would have it the young couple who purchased the property were local to the area, in fact the young woman was local to the village, a farmer's daughter, who was a distant relative! The young man and his brother had been friends of my husband in his village of North Ferriby and were now running their fathers very successful lighting business in Hull. Mill House would be in good hands, excellent hands as the young pair had enthusiasm and cash to do all the necessary renovations.

George and Kath moved into a cottage on the main road at Gilberdyke not far away from their son, his wife and their grandson Andrew, the cottages that Gracie Fields brother in law built!

Emily would have been pleased to see her beloved Mill House brought back to life so tastefully and lovingly. She would also have been pleased and tremendously proud of all her children and grand children's achievements, although I doubt that she would have understood our own sons commitment to the unity of Europe! The main aim of course being Peace. There is one thing that I am sure of Saskia, and that is that she would have adored her English, Dutch, Austrian great, great grand daughter as much we all do.

I hope that Mill House will stand proudly for many more years and that one day you will see the Leighton family home for yourself,   remembering proudly your fore bearers with their strong characters, stubborn determination and most importantly their ability to be full of fun and laughter what ever the situation.

Sadly I didn't meet my grandmother and yet I have always felt her presence in the family. The lasting memories she bequeathed to her children were so strong that she lived on, loved and admired by them all.

It would be wonderful to think that the love in our family could equal this, I am sure that it can.

WRITTEN WITH LOVE, FOR OUR BEAUTIFUL SASKIA.